THE ALLURE OF HORSES

THE ALLURE OF HORSES

PHOTOGRAPHS BY BOB LANGRISH

WILLOW CREEK PRESS

© 2005 Willow Creek Press
Photographs © Bob Langrish

See page 160 for Permissions Acknowledgments.

Published by Willow Creek Press
P.O. Box 147, Minocqua, WI 54548

Compiled by Andrea Donner

Library of Congress Cataloging-in-Publication Data:

The allure of horses.
        p. cm.
    ISBN 1-59543-152-7 (hardcover : alk. paper)
    1. Horses--Anecdotes. I. Willow Creek Press.
    SF301.A45 2005
    636.1--dc22

                        2005006855

Printed in the United States of America

Contents

THE ALLURE OF HORSES

MARGOT PAGE

◆ ◆ ◆

It would not be an exaggeration to say there are a million young girls and boys across the world day-dreaming this very instant about galloping a horse across a landscape, the thrill of the animal's speed and strength beneath them creating a rising bubble of joy in their hearts.

Or else they're dreaming about sharing a quiet moment with a hungry pony and a carrot.

Or imagining an arcing stream of water sluicing away dark sweat from the magnificent sculpture of the horse's body as defined in glistening, wet detail.

These are the images that horse-crazy people like myself carry with us, even into adulthood: the unknown adventure that beckons when a leafy trail unfolds between the eagerly pricked ears of your mount, your fellow pilgrim. Or the peace that envelops you when perched on an upside-down bucket in a stall, listening to the lazy munch of hay, a moment of respite in a busy adult world.

All of us know who we are. We are horse nuts—whether we get a lump in our throats watching a supreme equine athlete run his great, glorious heart out on a racetrack, feel a soaring sense of liberation when a pastured horse capers and gyrates in a coltish, awesome display of pure animal release—or whether we just experience a private, holy moment of communion with a large beast.

We all share a mythical, spiritual connection with this magnificent, breathtaking creature known as the horse... ancient symbol of myth and realism, elegance and rawness, sublime beauty and transcendent power, control and freedom.

Just listen to the storied legends of history and literature:

Pegasus. Bucephalus. The Trojan horse.

Black Beauty, Ginger, and Merrylegs. Flicka. Black Gold. Misty of Chincoteague. Stormy. The Black and Napolian. National Velvet.

Man o' War. War Admiral. Whirlaway. Citation. And perhaps the greatest race horse of all time, Secretariat.

Their very names bring chills of awe or a rush of warm memory. They take flight in our collective imaginations, these fabled horses of myth and lore.

I, too, was one of the legions of dreamy, horse-crazy kids—collecting the ubiquitous horse statues, studying the various breeds (and finally settling on the Palomino as the most beautiful and romantic of all), jamming the rigid plastic legs of my Barbie astride my plas-tic herd, and looping ordinary belts around my four-poster bed so that I could imagine I was driving a team of horses and a wagon train through a terrible storm. My obsession with horses became well-known to my sixth-grade teacher, who always kindly selected me to read aloud any passage that mentioned the "H" word. When my mother bribed me into getting another dreaded pixie hair cut with an offer of weekly riding lessons, her shameless negotiation was met with utter joy.

Then came magic years of hanging around the back-country Greenwich, Connecticut, stable where Foxtrot, Mr. Chips, Hopscotch, Butterscotch, and Coppertone stoically tolerated the daily bouncing of kids on their backs and I learned to ride. The heady smells of the barn, the sweet hay, candylike grain, even the distinctive odors of manure and horse sweat signaled my entrance into a safe, delicious, golden world, a world that was closer to the dreamworld where my true self lived than anything else in my life at the time. I withheld my barn clothes from the laundry for a few

extra days so as to prolong my contact with my private Eden and was an avid reader—at age twelve—of the weekly racing column in *The New Yorker*.

I never, however, owned my own horse until a decade later. After looking for hoofprints that failed to appear in my driveway for too many Christmas mornings, when finally an official adult, I gave myself the grandest present of all for my 21st birthday, a golden horse purchased for a princely sum of $800, which, by the way, I did not possess. Luckily, the seller took pity on an impoverished horse worshipper and the payment-plan route became a viable option.

Throughout the lean years of graduate school, I scrounged a way to hay, grain, and stable my buckskin horse, Carson, somehow always managing to locate funky farmhouses with old barns to rent. Carson was a stubborn, Roman-nosed Quarterhorse cross whose mouth was as hard as asphalt and who used to rocket me around the woods of New Hampshire. After a rather protracted and wild battle of wills, we eventually made our peace and there followed many wonderful adventures and journeys together. When he died in Maryland in 1982—mercifully, with one last clump of sweet grass in his mouth—one of the first victims of a then-new and unnamed virulent disease now known as Potomac Horse Fever, it was one of the saddest nights of my life.

It wasn't until nearly fifteen years later that a horse again came into my life, under unexpected circumstances. At a soccer game, I heard about a sweet and very large Thoroughbred mare being slowly starved to death who was destined to go the knackers if a home couldn't be found for her. I fell in love with her personality and her spidery hugeness, and a week later bought her for the price of her flesh.

Two hundred and fifty pounds later, Athena is a gorgeous, healthy animal who lives in a palace of a stable, who is doted on by her two humans—me and my 11-year-old daughter Brooke—and who brings home well-deserved blue ribbons.

When a horse gets wind under its tail, whether it be on the first crisp fall day or at the sight of a Really Scary Thing (be it a train, a cow, or a truly hideous piece of paper blowing across the paddock), nothing equals the momentary glory of its ballet: neck arched almost cobra-like, nostrils flared, eyes large and dark, tail up and streaming like the wind personified, delicate mane ribboning the air, and legs springing, their high action extended. The animal is suspended in air, its defined muscles rippling under its sleek coat.

No one witnessing these moments can do anything but stand, riveted, in silent awe of the sheer beauty of this dance.

◆ ◆ ◆

TALKING OF HORSES

MONICA DICKENS

♦ ♦ ♦

Long ago, five million years before the Stone Age, a horse was eohippus, 'the drawn horse', about the size and shape of a whippet, with toes. It grew larger and swifter, always running from its enemies, because it had no weapons to fight with. The side toes became shorter, and the middle toe developed into a hard hoof, drumming over the dry Mongolian steppes a million years ago.

Primitive men hunted this horse for food. Then some roaming, plundering tribesmen realised that they were eating an animal who could help them to roam farther and plunder more. Horses were pack animals at first. Five thousand years ago, they went to war, pulling chariots by awkward wooden yokes which pressed on the windpipe and jugular and made them throw up their heads. A horse can't pull fast with its head up, which is why it took four strong-necked stallions to pull one warrior in a two-wheeled chariot.

Then some inspired man saw the meaning of a horse's shape, and had the courage to jump on its back, and soon mounted swordsmen were riding rings round the unwieldy chariots. The Cavalry became supreme (it still takes precedence), the horse was admired and honoured, and the long, unending story of horse worship began.

To the Greeks, he was a god of beauty, half wild, half tame. Winged Pegasus, son of the goddess Medusa, carried the poets up to the firmament of fantasy. Poseidon the sea god sent forth the wonderful horse Arion, surging out of the foaming waves.

> Now the great winds seaward blow;
> Now the salt tides seaward flow;
> Now the wild white horses play,
> Champ and chafe and toss in the spray…

It was Hengist and Horsa who brought horses to Britain. That is why they are called horses. They brought horse worship too, and it stayed.

The spirit of that first man who had the vision to see why a horse was shaped like that, and the nerve to jump on its back and twist his fingers in its mane is still with us now, here where the horses are, sharing this strange, compelling partnership, working, or riding, or watching them over the gate of a field, chewing a blade of grass.

◆ ◆ ◆

RIDE BACK WITH ME

JESSIE HAAS

Saddle up,
  ride back with me.
  You take the Thoroughbred you have lessons on;
I'll ride my fat Morgan.
We'll travel past buckboard wagons, buffalo hunts,
  conquistadores, cavaliers,
  and every sort of infidel invader.
We'll skirt the edge of battlefields,
  follow the tinkling bells of pack trains.
Cling as your mount changes beneath you—
    hack, charger, destrier, rouncy, pad.
The stirrups will drop away,
  the girths will snap—
hold fast.
  At last we'll ride dun ponies,
    bareback
along the rims of glaciers.
While they are horses we will ride them.
Then we'll get off and walk,
  45 million years or so,
our brown-spotted companions
pattering beside us,
  on an ever-increasing number
    of toes.

The introduction of the horse by the Spaniards to the Native Americans revolutionized their existence. The Indians learned quickly and easily how to handle these powerful animals. With the horse, the Indians could either keep up with the buffalo herds or travel to them and hunt and return to camp by nightfall. Indians regularly stole horses from the Spaniards and traded them between tribes. Soon horses became a symbol of power and importance. Each tribe created its own legend of how it first received the horse.

The Making of Men and Horses
Assiniboine Native Americans

◆ ◆ ◆

Like other North American tribes, the Assiniboine did not have horses in any number until the eighteenth century, and yet they still credit the creation of horses to the wolf-god Inktonmi in the beginning of the world. The overwhelming importance of horses to relatively modern Assiniboine culture is thus expressed mythologically as essential, original, and determined from the start.

All the earth was flooded with water. Inktonmi sent animals to dive for dirt at the bottom of the sea. No animals was able to get any. At last he sent the Muskrat. It came up dead, but with dirt in its claws. Inktonmi saw the dirt, took it, and made the earth out of it.

Inktonmi was wearing a wolf-skin robe. He said, "There shall be as many months as there are hairs on this skin before it shall be summer." Frog said, "If the winter lasts as long as that, no creature will be able to live. Seven months of winter will be enough." He kept on repeating this, until Inktonmi got angry, and killed him. Still Frog stuck out seven of his toes. Finally, Inktonmi consented, and said there should be seven winter months.

Inktonmi then created men and horses out of dirt. Some of the Assiniboine and other northern tribes had no horses. Inktonmi told the Assiniboine that they were always to steal horses from other tribes.

◆ ◆ ◆

The Navajo of Arizona tell how the Sun (Johano-ai) leaves his hogan in the east and rides across the skies to his hogan in the west every day, carrying a shining, golden disk. He has five horses, all different colors. When Johano-ai rides his turquoise horse or his horse of white shell or pearl, the skies are blue with white clouds scuttling across. When he rides the red horse or the horse of coal, the skies are laden with storm clouds.

WAS THERE A HORSE WITH WINGS?

BERYL MARKHAM

♦ ♦ ♦

The black book lies on my father's desk, thick and important. Its covers are a little bent; the weight of his fingers and mine have curled back its pages, but they are not yellow. The handwriting is bold—in places it is even proud as when he has inscribed such names as these: 'Little Miller—Ormolu—Véronique.' They are all Thoroughbred mares out of stock old as boulders on an English hill.

The name 'Coquette' is inscribed more soberly, with no flourish—almost with doubt. It is as if here is a girl, pretty as any, but brought by marriage into a family of respectability beyond her birth or farthest hopes.

The brief career of Coquette is, in fact, ever so slightly chequered; her background, while not obscure, suggests something less than the dazzling gentility of her stable-mates. Still, not to be English is hardly regarded as a fatal deficiency even by the English, though grave enough to warrant sympathy. Coquette is Abyssinian. She is small and golden yellow with a pure white mane and tail.

Coquette was smuggled out of Abyssinia because Abyssinians do not permit good native mares to leave their country. I do not remember who did the smuggling, but I suppose my father condoned it, in effect, when he bought her. He must have done it with one eye shut and the other on the sweet, tidy lines of her vigorous body.

My father was, and is, a law-abiding citizen of the realm, but if ever he wanders off the path of righteousness, it will not be gold or silver

that enticed him, but, more likely, I think, the irresistible contours of a fine but elusive horse.

A lovely horse is always an experience to him. It is an emotional experience of the kind that is spoiled by words. He has always talked about horses, but he has never unravelled his love of them in a skein of commonplace adjectives. At seventy, in competition with the crack trainers of South Africa, his name heads the list of winners in the high-stake racing centre of Durban. In view of this and other things, I demand forgiveness for being so obviously impressed with my own parent.

He came out of Sandhurst with such a ponderous knowledge of Greek and Latin that it would have submerged a lesser man. He might have gone down like a swimmer in the sea struggling with an Alexandrian tablet under each arm, but he never let his education get the better of him. He won what prizes there were translating Ovid and Aeschylus, and then took up steeplechasing until he became one of the finest amateur riders in England. He took chances on horses and on Africa; he never regretted the losses, nor boasted about the wins.

He sometimes dreamed over the thick black book—almost as I am dreaming now, now that the names are just names, and the great-grandchildren of those elegant dams and sterling sires are dispersed, like a broken family.

But all great characters come back to life if you call them—even great horses.

Coquette, in her way, was great. She won races, though she never set the world agog, but she gave me my first foal.

It all goes back to the thick black book. And that is a long way back.

It lies there, dustless, because it is too much touched, and I am grown a little now and charged with duties inflexible as a drill sergeant's, but more pleasant. I have a corporal in Kibii, but he is often away from the farm these days, engaged in new and enigmatic offices.

My personal staff still numbers two—lean Otieno and fat, fat Toombo.

It is a morning in November. Some places in the world are grey as a northern sea in

November, and colder. Some are silver with ice. But not Njoro. In November, Njoro and all the Highlands await their ration of warm soft rain tendered regularly by one or another of the Native Gods—Kikuyu, Masai, Kavirondo—or by the White Man's God, or perhaps by all known Gods, working amiably together. November is a month of benison and birth.

I open the black book and run my finger down one of its freshest pages. I come to Coquette.

The book says:

COQUETTE

Date of Service	Stallion
20/1/1917	*Referee*

Eleven months for a mare. Bred to Referee—small, perfect, gallant as a warrior, smooth as a coin—Coquette is due to foal in a matter of days. I close the book and call for Toombo.

He comes—rather, he appears; he is a visitation in ebony. Nothing in this world of extremes is blacker than Toombo, nothing is rounder than his belly, nothing is broader than his smile. Toombo is the good jinn—the one that never got locked in the pot. He suddenly fills the doorway as if he had been set into it like a polished stone into a trinket.

'Do you want me, Beru—or is it Otieno?'

No matter how many times the name Beryl goes in the Native or Indian ear, it emerges from the lips—Beru. No English word is so smooth that the tongue trained to Swahili cannot make it smoother.

'I want both of you, Toombo. The day for Coquette is very near. We must begin the watch.'

Toombo's grin spreads over his wide face like a ripple in a pond. To him, birth and success are synonymous; the hatching of a hen's egg is a triumph, or even the bursting of a seed. Toombo's own birth is the major success of his life. He grins until there is no more room for both the grin and his eyes, so his eyes disappear. He turns and shuffles through the doorway and I hear his deep voice bawling for Otieno.

The missionaries have already pitched their tents in the Kavirondo country, which is Otieno's home. They have jousted with the old black gods and even unhorsed a few. They have traded

a tangible Bible for a handful of intangible super-
stitions—the Kavirondo mind is fertile ground.

Otieno's Bible (translated into Jaluo, which
he reads) has made him both a Christian and a
night-owl. Night after night he sits in the yellow
circle of his hurricane lamp and squints over the
pages. He is indefatigable, sleepless, dependable
as daylight—and half a mystic. I let him under-
take, with Toombo, the night-watch in
Coquette's box, knowing that he never nods.

He accepts the duty with pious gravity—as
indeed he should. Tall and sombre-eyed, he
stands where Toombo stood. If it were not
morning, and if there were no work to be done,
and if it were not my father's study, Otieno
would sheepishly stroke the calf of his black
leg with the sole of his black foot and tell me
the story of Lot's wife.

'I have been reading in the Book,' he would
begin, 'about a strange happening…'

But something more common, though
perhaps as strange, is near its happening, and
Otieno leaves and I close the black book and
follow him down to the stables.

Ah, Coquette! How could a creature deserving such a gay name have become so dowdy? Once she was small and pert and golden, but now she is plain and shapeless with the weight of her foal. Her thin pasterns are bent with it until her fetlocks seem ready to touch the ground; her hooves are of lead. She has seen so much—the savage hills and plains of Abyssinia, all that wild and deep country on the way to Njoro, all those different people, those different races, those different rocks and trees. Coquette has seen the world, but the bright, wise eyes are not now so bright. Soon they will be wiser.

Her foaling-box is ready. Her body-brush, her dandy-brush, and her kitamba are there. Her coat is still no other colour than gold, her mane and her tail are still white silk. The gold is tarnished; the silk lacks lustre. Coquette looks at me as she enters the box—to wait, and wait.

All of us there—Toombo, Otieno, and myself—know the secret. We know what Coquette is waiting for, but she does not. None of us can tell her.

Toombo and Otieno begin their nightly watch. And the time goes slowly.

But there are other things. Everything else goes on as it always has. Nothing is more common than birth; a million creatures are born in the time it takes to turn this page, and another million die. The symbolism is commonplace; countless dreamers have played countless tunes upon the mystery, but horse-breeders are realists and every farmer is a midwife. There is no time for mystery. There is only time for patience and care, and hope that what is born is worthy and good.

I do not know why most foals are born at night, but most of them are. This one is.

Nineteen long days pass, and on the evening of the twentieth, I make the rounds of the stables, as usual, ending at Coquette's foaling-box. Buller is at my heels. Otieno The Vigilant is there—and Toombo The Rotund.

The hurricane lamp has already been lighted inside the foaling-box. It is a large box, large as a room, with walls of cedar planking milled on the farm. The floor is earthen, cov-

ered with deep grass bedding gathered fresh from the pastures; the smell of a mowed field is gathered with it.

Coquette stands heavily under the gentle glow of the lamp, her evening feed not finished. Creating new life within her, she is herself almost lifeless. She lowers her head as if it were not the exquisitely fashioned head that it is, but an ugly and tiresome burden. She nibbles at a single leaf of lucerne, too small to be tasted, then shambles on sluggish feet across the box. To her all things are poignantly lacking—but she is incapable of desiring anything.

Otieno sighs. Toombo's face beams back at the hurricane lamp, matching its glow with his glow. Outside the box, Buller challenges the oncoming night with a softly warning growl.

I bend down and lay my head against the smooth, warm belly of the mare. The new life is there. I hear and feel it, struggling already— demanding the right to freedom and growth. I hope it is perfect; I hope it is strong. It will not, at first, be beautiful.

I turn from Coquette to Otieno. 'Watch carefully. It is near.'

The tall, thin Kavirondo looks into the face of the fat one. Toombo's face is receptive—it cannot be looked at, it can only be looked into. It is a jovial and capacious bowl, often empty, but not now. Now it is filled to the brim with expectation. 'This is a good night,' he says, 'this is a good night.' Well, perhaps he is optimistic, but it proves a busy night.

I return to my hut—my new, proud hut which my father has built for me out of cedar, with real shingles instead of thatch. In it I have my first glass window, my first wood floor—and my first mirror. I have always known what I looked like—but at fifteen-odd, I become curious to know what can be done about it. Nothing, I suppose—and who would there be to know the difference? Still, at that age, few things can provoke more wonderment than a mirror.

At eight-thirty Otieno knocks.

'Come quickly. She is lying.'

Knives, twine, disinfectant—even anaesthetic—are all ready in my foaling-kit, but the last is precaution. As an Abyssinian, Coquette should have few of the difficulties that so often attend a thoroughbred mare. Still, this is Coquette's first. First things are not always easy. I snatch the kit and hurry through the cluster of huts, some dark and asleep, some wakeful with square, yellow eyes. Otieno at my heels, I reach the stable.

Coquette is down. She is flat on her side, breathing in spasmodic jerks. Horses are not voiceless in pain. A mare in the throes of birth is almost helpless, but she is able to cry out her agony. Coquette's groans, deep, tired, and a little frightened, are not really violent. They are not hysterical, but they are infinitely expressive of suffering, because they are unanswerable.

I kneel in the grass bedding and feel her soft ears. They are limp and moist in the palm of my hand, but there is no temperature. She labours heavily, looking at nothing out of staring eyes. Or perhaps she is seeing her own pain dance before them.

The time is not yet. We cannot help, but we can watch. We three can sit cross-legged—Toombo near the manger, Otieno against the cedar planking, myself near the heavy head of

Coquette—and we can talk, almost tranquilly, about other things while the little brush of flame in the hurricane lamp paints experimental pictures on the wall.

'Wa-li-hie!' says Toombo.

It is as solemn as he ever gets. At the dawning of doomsday he will say no more. A single 'Walihie!' and he has shot his philosophic bolt. Having shot it, he relaxes and grins, genially, into himself.

The labouring of Coquette ebbs and flows in methodical tides of torment. There are minutes of peace and minutes of anguish, which we all feel together, but smother, for ourselves, with words.

Otieno sighs. 'The Book talks of many strange lands,' he says. 'There is one that is filled with milk and with honey. Do you think this land would be good for a man, Beru?'

Toombo lifts his shoulders. 'For which man?' he says. 'Milk is not bad food for one man, meat is better for another, *ooji* is good for all. Myself, I do not like honey.'

Otieno's scowl is mildly withering. 'Whatever you like, you like too much, Toombo. Look at the roundness of your belly. Look at the heaviness of your legs!'

Toombo looks. 'God makes fat birds and small birds, trees that are wide and trees that are thin, like wattle. He makes big kernels and little kernels. I am a big kernel. One does not argue with God.'

The theosophism defeats Otieno; he ignores the globular Jesuit slouching unperturbed under the manger, and turns again to me.

'Perhaps you have seen this land, Beru?'

'No.' I shake my head.

But then I am not sure. My father has told me that I was four when I left England.

Leicestershire. Conceivably it could be the land of milk and honey, but I do not remember it as such. I remember a ship that sailed interminably up the hill of the sea and never, never reached the top. I remember a place I was later taught to think of as Mombasa, but the name has not explained the memory. It is a simple memory made only of colours and shapes, of heat and trudging people and broad-leaved trees that looked cooler than they were. All the country I know is this country—these hills, familiar as an old wish, this veldt, this forest. Otieno knows as much.

'I have never seen such a land, Otieno. Like you, I have read about it. I do not know where it is or what it means.'

'That is a sad thing,' says Otieno; 'it sounds like a good land.'

Toombo rouses himself from the stable floor and shrugs. 'Who would walk far for a kibuyu of milk and a hive of honey? Bees live in every tenth tree, and every cow has four teats. Let us talk of better things!'

But Coquette talks first of better things. She groans suddenly from the depth of her womb, and trembles. Otieno reaches at once for the hurricane lamp and swells the flame with a twist of his black fingers. Toombo opens the foaling-kit.

'Now.' Coquette says it with her eyes and with her wordless voice. 'Now—perhaps now'

This is the moment, and the Promised Land is the forgotten one.

I kneel over the mare waiting for her foal to make its exit from oblivion. I wait for the first glimpse of the tiny hooves, the first sight of the sheath—the cloak it will wear for its great début.

It appears, and Coquette and I work together. Otieno at one of my shoulders, Toombo at the other. No one speaks because there is nothing to say.

But there are things to wonder.

Will this be a colt or a filly? Will it be sound and well-formed? Will its new heart be strong and stubborn enough to snap the tethers of nothingness that break so grudgingly? Will it breathe when it is meant to breathe? Will it have the anger to feed and to grow and to demand its needs?

I have my hands at last on the tiny legs, on the bag encasing them. It is a strong bag, transparent and sleek. Through it I see the diminutive hooves, pointed, soft as the flesh of sprouted seeds—impotent hooves, insolent in their urgency to tread the tough earth.

Gently, gently, but strong and steady, I coax the new life into the glow of the stable lamp, and the mare strains with all she has. I renew my grip, hand over hand, waiting for her muscles to surge with my pull. The nose—the head, the whole head—at last the foal itself, slips into my arms, and the silence that follows is sharp as the crack of a Dutchman's whip—and as short.

'Walihie!' says Toombo.

Otieno smears sweat from under his eyes; Coquette sighs the last pain out of her.

I let the shining bag rest on the pad of trampled grass less than an instant, then break it, giving full freedom to the wobbly little head.

I watch the soft, mouse-coloured nostrils suck at their first taste of air. With care, I slip the whole bag away, tie the cord and cut it with the knife Otieno hands me. The old life of the mare and the new life of the foal for the last time run together in a quick christening of blood, and as I bathe the wound with disinfectant, I see that he is a colt.

He is a strong colt, hot in my hands and full of the tremor of living.

Coquette stirs. She knows now what birth is; she can cope with what she knows. She lurches to her feet without gracefulness or balance, and whinnies once—so this is mine! So this is what I have borne! Together we dry the babe.

When it is done, I stand up and turn to smile at Otieno. But it is not Otieno; it is not Toombo. My father stands beside me with the air of a man who has observed more than anyone suspected. This is a scene he has witnessed more times than he can remember; yet there is bright interest in his eyes—as if, after all these years, he has at last seen the birth of a foal!

He is not a short man nor a tall one; he is lean and tough as a riem. His eyes are dark and kind in a rugged face that can be gentle.

'So there you are,' he says—'a fine job of work and a fine colt. Shall I reward you or Coquette—or both?'

Toombo grins and Otieno respectfully

scuffs the floor with his toes. I slip my arm through my father's and together we look down on the awkward, angry little bundle, fighting already to gain his feet.

'Render unto Caesar,' says my father; 'you brought him to life. He shall be yours.'

A bank clerk handles pounds of gold—none of it his own—but if, one day, that fabulous faery everyone expects, but nobody ever meets, were to give him all this gold for himself—or even a part of it—he would be no less overjoyed because he had looked at it daily for years. He would know at once (if he hadn't known it before) that this was what he had always wanted.

For years I had handled my father's horses, fed them, ridden them, groomed them, and loved them. But I had never owned one.

Now I owned one. Without even the benefit of the good fairy, but only because my father said so, I owned one for myself. The colt was to be mine, and no one could ever touch him, or ride him, or feed him, or nurse him—no one except myself.

I do not remember thanking my father; I suppose I did, for whatever words are worth. I remember that when the foaling-box was cleaned, the light turned down again, and Otieno left to watch over the newly born, I went out and walked with Buller beyond the stables and a little way down the path that used to lead to Arab Maina's.

I thought about the new colt, Otieno's Promised Land, how big the world must be, and then about the colt again. What shall I name him?

Who doesn't look upward when searching for a name? Looking upward, what is there but the sky to see? And seeing it, how can the name or the hope be earthbound? Was there a horse named Pegasus that flew? Was there a horse with wings?

Yes, once there was—once, long ago, there was. And now there is again.

◆ ◆ ◆

THE CHIMAERA

NATHANIEL HAWTHORNE

◆ ◆ ◆

Once, in the old, old times (for all the strange things which I tell you about happened long before anybody can remember), a fountain gushed out of a hillside, in the marvelous land of Greece. And, for aught I know, after so many thousand years, it is still gushing out of the very self-same spot. At any rate, there was the pleasant fountain, welling freshly forth and sparkling adown the hillside, in the golden sunset, when a handsome young man named Bellerophon drew near its margin. In his hand he held a bridle studded with brilliant gems, and adorned with a golden bit. Seeing an old man, and another of middle age, and a little boy, near the fountain, and likewise a maiden, who was dipping up some of the water in a pitcher, he paused, and begged that he might refresh himself with a draught.

"This is very delicious water," he said to the maiden as he rinsed and filled her pitcher, after drinking out of it. "Will you be kind enough to tell me whether the fountain has a name?"

"Yes, it is called the Fountain of Pirene," answered the maiden; and then she added, "My grandmother has told me that this clear fountain was once a beautiful woman, and when her son was killed by the arrow of the huntress Diana, she melted all away into tears. And so the water, which you find so cool and sweet, is the sorrow of that poor mother's heart!"

"I should have not dreamed," observed the young stranger, "that so clear a wellspring, with its gush and gurgle, and its cheery dance out of the shade into the sunlight, had so much as one teardrop in its bosom! And this, then, is Pirene! I thank you, pretty maiden, for telling me its name. I have come from a faraway country to find this very spot."

A middle-aged country fellow (he had driven his cow to drink out of the spring) stared hard at young Bellerophon, and at the handsome bridle which he carried in his hand.

"The watercourses must be getting low, friend, in your part of the world," remarked he, "if you come so far only to find the Fountain of Pirene. But, pray, have you lost a horse? I see you carry the bridle in your hand; and a pretty one it is, with that double row of bright stones upon it. If the horse was as fine as the bridle, you are much to be pitied for losing him."

"I have lost no horse," said Bellerophon, with a smile. "But I happen to be seeking a very famous one, which, as wise people have informed me, must be found hereabouts, if anywhere. Do you know whether the winged horse

Pegasus still haunts the Fountain of Pirene, as he used to do in your forefathers' day?"

But then the country fellow laughed.

Some of you, my little friends, have probably heard that this Pegasus was a snow-white steed, with beautiful silvery wings, who spent most of his time on the summit of Mount Helicon. He was as wild, and as swift, and as buoyant, in his flight through the air, as any eagle that ever soared into the clouds. There was nothing else like him in the world. He had no mate; he had never been backed or bridled by a master; and for many a long year, he led a solitary and happy life.

Oh, how fine a thing it is to be a winged horse! Sleeping at night, as he did, on a lofty mountaintop, and passing the greater part of the day in the air, Pegasus seemed hardly to be a creature of the earth. Whenever he was seen, up very high above people's heads, with the sunshine on his silvery wings, you would have thought that he belonged to the sky, and that, skimming a little too low, he had got astray among our mists and vapors, and was seeking

his way back again. It was very pretty to behold him to plunge into the fleecy bosom of a bright cloud, and be lost in it for a moment or two, and then break forth from the other side. Or, in a sullen rainstorm, when there was a grey pavement of clouds over the whole sky, it would sometimes happen that the winged horse descended right through it, and the glad light of the upper region would gleam after him. In another instant, it is true, both Pegasus and the pleasant light would be gone away together. But anyone who was fortunate enough to see this wondrous spectacle felt cheerful the whole day afterwards, and as much longer as the storm lasted.

In the summertime, and in the beautifullest of weather, Pegasus often alighted on the solid earth, and, closing his silvery wings, would gallop over hill and dale for pastime, as fleetly as the wind. Oftener than in any other place, he had been seen near the Fountain of Pirene, drinking the delicious water, or rolling himself across the soft grass of the margin. Sometimes, too (but Pegasus was very dainty in his food),

he would crop a few of the clover blossoms that happened to be the sweetest.

To the Fountain of Pirene, therefore, people's great-grandfathers had been in the habit of going (as long as they were youthful, and retained their faith in the winged horses), in hopes of getting a glimpse at the beautiful Pegasus. But, of late years, he had been very seldom seen. Indeed, there were many of the country folks, dwelling within half an hour's walk of the fountain, who had never beheld Pegasus, and did not believe that there was any such creature in existence. The country fellow to whom Bellerophon was speaking chanced to be one of those incredulous persons.

And that was the reason he laughed.

"Pegasus indeed!" cried he, turning up his nose as high as such a flat nose could be turned up, "Pegasus, indeed! A winged horse truly! Why, friend, are you in your senses? Of what use would wings be to a horse? Could he drag the plough so well, think you? To be sure, there might be a little saving in the expense of shoes, but then, how would a man like to see his horse flying out of the stable window?—Yes, or whisking him above the clouds, when he only wanted to ride to mill? No, no! I don't believe in Pegasus. There never was such a ridiculous kind of horse-fowl made!"

"I have some reason to think otherwise," said Bellerophon, quietly.

And then he turned to the old, grey man, who was leaning on a staff, and listening very attentively, with his head stretched forward, and one hand at his ear, because, for the last twenty years, he had been getting rather deaf.

"And what do you say, venerable sir?" inquired he. "In your younger days, I should imagine, you must frequently have seen the winged steed!"

"Ah, young stranger, my memory is very poor!" said the aged man. "When I was a lad, if I remember rightly, I used to believe there was such a horse, and so did everbody else. But, nowadays, I hardly know what to think, and very seldom think about the winged horse at all. If I ever saw the creature, it was a long, long while ago; and to tell you the truth, I doubt whether I ever did see him. One day, to be sure, when I was quite a youth, I remember seeing some hoof-tramps round about the brink of the fountain. Pegasus might have made those hoof-marks; and so might some other horse."

"And have you never seen him, my fair maiden?" asked Bellerophon of the girl, who stood with the pitcher on her head, while this talk went on. "You certainly could see Pegasus, if anybody can, for your eyes are very bright."

"Once I thought I saw him," replied the maiden, with a smile and a blush. "It was either Pegasus, or a large white bird, a very great way up in the air. And one other time, as I was coming to the fountain with my pitcher, I heard a neigh. Oh, such a brisk and melodious neigh as that was! My very heart leaped with delight at the sound. But, it startled me, nevertheless, so that I ran home without filling my pitcher."

"That was truly a pity," said Bellerophon.

And he turned to the child, whom I mentioned at the beginning of the story, and who was gazing at him, as children are apt to gaze at strangers, with his rosy mouth wide open.

"Well, my little fellow," cried Bellerophon, playfully pulling one of his curls, "I suppose you have often seen the winged horse."

"That I have," answered the child very readily. "I saw him yesterday, and many times before."

"You are a fine little man!" said Bellerophon, drawing the child closer to him. "Come, tell me all about it."

"Why," replied the child, "I often come here to sail little boats in the fountain, and to gather pretty pebbles out of its basin. And sometimes, when I look down into the water, I see the image of the winged horse, in the picture of the sky that is there. I wish he would come down and take me on his back, and let me ride him up to the moon! But, if I so much as stir to look at him, he flies far away out of sight."

And Bellerophon put his faith in the child, who had seen the image of Pegasus in the water, and in the maiden who had heard him neigh so melodiously, rather than in the middle-aged clown, who believed only in cart horses, or in the old man who had forgotten the beautiful things of his youth.

Therefore, he haunted about the Fountain of Pirene for a great many days afterwards. He kept continually on the watch, looking upward at the sky, or else down into the water, hoping forever that he should see either the reflected image of the winged horse, or the marvelous reality. He held the bridle, with its bright gems and golden bit, always ready in his hand. The rustic people, who dwelt in the neighborhood, and drove their cattle to the fountain to drink, would often laugh at poor Bellerophon, and sometimes take him pretty severely to task. They told him that an ablebodied young man, like himself, ought to have better business than to be wasting his time in such idle pursuit. They offered to sell him a horse, if he wanted one; and when Bellerophon declined the purchase, they tried to drive a bargain with him for his fine bridle.

Even the country boys thought him so very foolish that they used to have a great deal of sport about him, and were rude enough not to care a fig, although Bellerophon saw and heard it. One little urchin, for example, would play Pegasus, and cut the oddest imaginable capers, by way of flying; while one of his schoolfellows would scamper after him holding forth a twist of bulrushes, which was intended to represent Bellerophon's ornamental bridle. But the gentle child, who had seen the picture of Pegasus in the water, comforted the young stranger more than all the naughty boys could torment him. The dear little fellow, in his play hours, often sat down beside him, and without speaking a word, would look down into the fountain and up towards the sky, with so innocent a faith, that Bellerophon could not help feeling encouraged.

Well was it for Bellerophon that the child had grown so fond of him, and was never weary of keeping him company. Every morning the child gave him a new hope to put in his bosom, instead of yesterday's withered one.

"Dear Bellerophon," he would cry, looking up hopefully into his face, "I think we shall see Pegasus today!"

One morning the child spoke to Bellerophon even more hopefully than usual.

"Dear, dear Bellerophon," cried he, "I know not why it is, but I feel as if we shall certainly see Pegasus today!"

And all that day he would not stir a step from Bellerophon's side; so they ate a crust of bread together, and drank some of the water from the fountain. In the afternoon, there they sat, and Bellerophon had thrown his arm around the child, who likewise had put one of his little hands into Bellerophon's. The latter was lost in his own thoughts, and was fixing his eyes vacantly on the trunks of the trees that overshadowed the fountain, and on the grapevines that clambered up among the branches. But the gentle child was gazing down into the water. He was grieved, for Bellerophon's sake, that the hope of another day should be deceived, like so many before it; and two or three quiet teardrops fell from his eyes, and mingled with what were said to be the many tears of Pirene, when she wept for her slain children.

But, when he least thought of it, Bellerophon felt the pressure of the child's little hand, and heard a soft, almost breathless whisper.

"See there, dear Bellerophon, there is an image in the water!"

The young man looked down into the dimpling mirror of the fountain, and saw what he took to be the reflection of a bird which seemed to be flying at a great height in the air, with a gleam of sunshine on its snowy or silvery wings.

"What a splendid bird it must be!" said he. "And how very large it looks, though it must really be flying higher than the clouds!"

"It makes me tremble!" whispered the child. "I am afraid to look up into the air! It is very beautiful, and yet I dare only look at its image in the water. Dear Bellerophon, do you not see that it is not bird? It is the winged horse Pegasus!"

Bellerophon's heart began to throb! He gazed keenly upward, but could not see the winged creature, whether bird or horse; because, just then, it had plunged into the fleecy depths of a summer cloud. It was but a moment, however, before the object reappeared, sinking lightly down out of the cloud, although still a vast distance from the earth. Bellerophon caught the child in his arms, and shrank back with him, so that they were both hidden among the thick shrubbery which grew all around the fountain. Not that he was afraid of any harm, but he dreaded lest, if Pegasus caught a glimpse of them, he would fly far away, and alight in some inaccessible mountaintop. For it really was the winged horse. After they had expected him so long, he was coming to quench his thirst with the water of Pirene.

Nearer and nearer came the aerial wonder, flying in great circles, as you may have seen a dove when about to alight. Downward came Pegasus, in those wide, sweeping circles, which grew narrower, and narrower still, as he gradually approached the earth. The nigher the view of him, the more beautiful he was, and the more marvelous the sweep of his silvery wings. At last, with so slight a pressure as hardly to bend the grass about the fountain, or imprint a hoof-tramp in the sand of its margin, he alighted, and, stooping his wild head, began to drink. He drew in the water, with long and pleasant sighs, and tranquil pauses of enjoyment; and then another draught, and another, and another. For, nowhere in the world, or up among the clouds, did Pegasus love any water as he loved this of Pirene. And when his thirst was slaked, he cropped a few of the honey blossoms of the clover, delicately tasting them, but not caring to make a hearty meal, because the herbage, just beneath the clouds, on the lofty sides of Mount Helicon, suited his palate better than this ordinary grass.

After thus drinking to his heart's content, and in his dainty fashion, condescending to take a little food, the winged horse began to caper to and fro, and dance, as it were, out of mere idleness and sport. There was never a more playful creature made than this very Pegasus. So there he frisked, in a way that delights me to think about, fluttering his great wings as lightly as ever did a linnet, and running little races, half on earth and half in air, and which I know not whether to call a flight or a gallop. When a creature is perfectly able to fly, he sometimes chooses to run, just for the pastime of the thing; and so did Pegasus,

although it cost him some little trouble to keep his hoofs so near the ground. Bellerophon, meanwhile, holding the child's hand, peeped forth from the shrubbery, and thought that never was any sight so beautiful as this, nor ever a horse's eyes so wild and spirited as those of Pegasus. It seemed a sin to think of bridling him and riding on his back.

Once or twice, Pegasus stopped, and snuffed the air, pricking up his ears, tossing his head, and turning it on all sides, as if he partly suspected some mischief or other. Seeing nothing, however, and hearing no sound, he soon began his antics again.

At length—not that he was weary, but only idle and luxurious—Pegasus folded his wings, and lay down on the soft green turf. But, being too full of aerial life to remain quiet for many moments together, he soon rolled over on his back, with his four slender legs in the air. It was beautiful to see him, this one solitary creature, whose mate had never been created, but who needed no companion, and, living a great many hundred years, was as happy as the cen-

turies were long. The more he did such things as mortal horses are accustomed to do, the less earthly and the more wonderful he seemed. Bellerophon and the child almost held their breath, partly from a delightful awe, but still more because they dreaded lest the slightest stir or murmur should send him up, with the speed of an arrow-flight into the farthest blue of the sky.

Finally, when he had enough of rolling over and over, Pegasus turned himself about, and, indolently, like an other horse, put out his forelegs, in order to rise from the ground; and Bellerophon, who had guessed that he would do so, darted suddenly from the thicket, and leaped astride of his back.

Yes, there he sat, on the back of the winged horse!

But what a bound did Pegasus make, when, for the first time, he felt the weight of a mortal man upon his loins! A bound, indeed! Before he had time to draw a breath, Bellerophon found himself five hundred feet aloft, and still shooting upward, while the winged horse snorted and trembled with terror and anger. Upward he went, up, up, up, until he plunged into the cold misty bosom of a cloud, at which, only a little while before, Bellerophon had been gazing, and fancying it a very pleasant spot. Then again, out of the heart of the cloud, Pegasus shot down like a thunderbolt, as if he meant to dash both himself and his rider headlong against a rock. Then he went through about a thousand of the wildest caprioles that had ever been performed either by a bird or a horse.

I cannot tell you half that he did. He skimmed straightforward, and sideways, and backward. He reared himself erect, with his forelegs on a wreath of mist and his hind legs on nothing at all. He flung his heels behind, and put his head between his legs, with his wings pointing right upward. At about two miles' height above the earth, he turned a somerset, so that Bellerophon's heels were where his head should have been, and he seemed to look down into the sky, instead of up. He twisted his head about, and looking Bellerophon in the face, with fire flashing from his eyes, made a terrible attempt to bite him. He fluttered his pinions so wildly that one of the silver feathers was shaken out, and, floating earthward, was picked up by the child, who kept it as long as he lived, in memory of Pegasus and Bellerophon.

But the latter (who, as you may judge, was as good a horseman as ever galloped) had been watching his opportunity, and at last clapped the golden bit of the enchanted bridle between the winged steed's jaws. No sooner was this done, than Pegasus became as manageable as if he had taken food all his life out of Bellerophon's hand. To speak what I really feel, it was almost a sadness to see so wild a creature grow suddenly so tame. And Pegasus seemed to feel it so, likewise. He looked round to Bellerophon with tears in his beautiful eyes instead of the fire that so recently flashed from them. But when Bellerophon patted his head, and spoke a few authoritative, yet kind and soothing words; another look came into the eyes of Pegasus; for he was glad at heart, after so many lonely centuries, to have found a companion and a master.

Thus it always is with winged horses, and with all such wild and solitary creatures. If you can catch and overcome them, it is the surest way to win their love.

❖ ❖ ❖

MR. T'S HEART

JANE SMILEY

* * *

I always suspected Mr. T. had one of those large economy-size thoroughbred hearts: maybe not Secretariat size (twenty-two pounds) or Mill Reef size (seventeen pounds), but larger and stronger than average (seven pounds). The horse was a fitness machine.

In five years of riding and eventing, I had never tired him out. He was always ready for more, even if I was nearly falling off him from the exertion.

Every year at his well-horse checkup, the vet would comment on his dropped beats—he could drop two or even three (five seconds between two heartbeats seems like a very long time when the horse is standing before you, apparently alive and well)—and attrib-

ute it to the residual effect of a great deal of exercise early in life. (He was a racehorse for eight years and had fifty-two starts.) Thus it was that I wasn't too worried when this year, Mr. T.'s twenty-first, the vet detected what he called arrhythmia. As I was taking another horse up to the vet clinic at UC Davis anyway, I packed Mr. T. along.

The results weren't good. On the one hand, the senior cardiologist shook my hand and thanked me for bringing him a big, lean thoroughbred with a heart that was so efficient and powerful that through the stethoscope it was nearly deafening. On the other hand, that arrhythmia had a name. It was "atrial fibrillation"; and it wasn't just a quirk, it was a potentially dangerous condition. The horse could drop dead at any moment.

I was impressed in spite of myself (and in spite of my conviction that Mr. T. was going to live forever) and agreed to have him "converted"—that is, to allow the cardiologist to administer a powerful and toxic drug, quinidine, that might or might not convert his chaotic heart rhythm to a normal or "sinous" rhythm. It was an in-patient procedure. I left him there and brought my other horse home.

Mr. T. was a very bad patient. He wouldn't eat, wouldn't relax, would hardly drink. His separation anxiety was so great that the cardiologist actually feared for his survival. He did, however, "convert"—his heart rhythm returned to normal, without any dropped beats—and stayed converted.

The bad news was that the dose it had taken to convert him was very close to toxic. There would be no trying this again. And the quinidine took maybe twice as long to clear his system as usual, putting him at risk in other ways.

I tried not to pay attention to the cardiologist's other remark—that the longer the heart had been arrhythmic, the less likely a permanent conversion. Those dropped beats we had always heard—I wasn't going to admit the possibility that his heart had been arrhythmic as long as I had known him.

As some readers of this magazine may know, Mr. T. (profiled in November 1998's "Why I Can't Find a New Horse") had stopped being a jumper—age, an eye injury, and timidity on my part. But not long after I wrote about him, he started jumping again, and he was great at it, as he had once been—energetic, fast, and full of thrust. And there was no changing his go-for-it style. I'd tried that, and it had just made him confused and anxious. You couldn't parse a fence or a combination or a course and try to get him to jump in a relaxed, easy style. You had to sit up, hold on, and let him do it. It was hugely exciting.

Anyway, two weeks after the conversion, Mike, my local vet, took another EKG. Tick Tock Tick Tock (that was the horse's real

name), everything was perfect. I began conditioning Mr. T. for an event at the end of June.

I was well organized in my training, for once. I had him entered in a schooling show, in a couple of jumper classes, and I was galloping him at a local training track once a week. At the beginning of June, I took him over to the track, a half-mile oval. As soon as we entered the gate, he picked up a huge, even, ground-covering trot on very light contact. He trotted happily, his ears pricked, for two miles. Then I walked him half a mile and asked for the canter. For a mile, it was collected, even, easy, a perfect joy. Then I walked him again.

At the last, I gave in to impulse. After he had caught his breath, I turned him, bridged my reins, and assumed galloping position. I said out loud, "Pick your own pace," and he did. He took hold and shot forward, switching leads and going faster about every eighth of a mile, exactly like a racehorse. But then, he was always a racehorse. The other stuff was just for fun.

For me, the "breeze" was both frightening and exhilarating—as fast as I had ever gone on a horse, but incredibly stable. Yes, I was not in control, but he was, and I never doubted that he knew exactly where each foot was at every stride. More important, all this exercise was effortless. He was hardly blowing after we had gone half a mile and I managed to bring him down. It took him the usual ten minutes to cool out.

Three days later, we went to the show. He warmed up and jumped around perfectly, won a couple of ribbons, seemed happy.

Thus it was that I couldn't believe it, four days after that, when Mike told me that his atrial fibrillation was back, and possibly worse. His heart rhythm was chaotic. We took another EKG, sent it off to Davis, discussed it more than necessary with lots of vets. The cardiologist's recommendation was discouraging—walking around, maybe a little trotting from time to time. But, I said. But. But when I galloped him on the track, the work was effortless for him.

The answer to the riddle was in his large, strong heart. He had enough overcapacity to give himself some leeway, to oxygenate himself thoroughly almost all of the time. The danger, to me as well as to him, was that his overcapacity was unpredictable. He could literally be doing fine one moment and drop dead the next. And, the cardiologist suggested, in accordance with the no-free-lunch principle, greater-than-average heart size often went with arrhythmia. His recommendation stayed the same—walking, a little jogging from time to time.

I stopped riding the horse. I'm not sure why, except that I was confused and ambivalent. One day I decided to ignore the cardiologist's advice, the next day I decided to heed it. Mr. T. and I were used to working, and working pretty hard. If we weren't allowed to work hard together, then what? I didn't know. I let him hang out in the pasture with his broodmare friend.

Not too long ago, I decided to pretty much ignore the cardiologist. I wouldn't be stupid and run Mr. T. cross-country or "breeze" him again, but I would do dressage and jump and treat him like a normal horse.

That very day, I went out to give him a carrot, and he was standing in the shade, pawing the ground. I put him in a stall with lots of water and no food—he'd been colicky before. By bedtime, he had manured three or four times.

In the morning he seemed right as rain, so I began introducing a bit of hay. He continued to seem fine. After noon, I let him out. An hour later, he was pawing and looking at his flanks. I called Mike, who was engaged but promised to come ASAP.

Half an hour later, the horse was eating manure. My heart sank. Even though Mike and another vet I asked said this meant nothing with regard to colic, I knew differently. I had never seen him do such a thing, and I thought it was an act of equine desperation.

The rest of the day was a losing battle. No matter how much painkiller of whatever kind we gave him, the pain could not be alleviated. And his atrial fibrillation meant that he could not tolerate surgery. The impaction, which may or may not have been a torsion, was out of reach and would not dissolve. At 10:00 p.m., I said to Mike, "Are you telling me now's the time?"

He said, "Yes."

I led Mr. T. out of the lighted stall where we had been trying to treat him. He moved, but his head was down and he was hardly conscious of me. We went out into the grassy pasture where he had wandered at large every day of the spring. I knelt down in front of my horse's lowered head, and I told him what a wonderful horse he was, perfect from top to toe every minute. Then Mike gave him the two big shots of barbiturates that would cause him to arrest.

Arrest what?

His heart.

It didn't take more than a second or two. Mike held the lead rope. The collapse of a horse is always earth-shaking. His haunches drop backward, his head flies up, his knees buckle, he fells to the side. We flocked around him, petting and talking to him, but he was gone already.

After everyone left, my boyfriend and I covered him with blankets and went in the house.

I slept fitfully, unable to grasp the suddenness and enormity of the death of my dear friend and constant companion. Each time I woke up, I dreaded going out there at daybreak—what would he look like? How would the mare be acting? What would I do next with a thirteen-hundred-pound body?

When it was finally time to get up, my boyfriend got up with me, and we went out. The mare was in her stall, quiet. I fed her. Then we approached the mound. Fermentation from the impacted food had already begun—under the blanket, my horse's belly was beginning visibly to swell.

I folded back the cover, expecting something horrible, but Mr. T.'s eyes were closed—a kindness my boyfriend had done me the night before. I can't express how important this was. It was not that I had ever seen his eyes closed before. I had not—he was too alert to sleep in my presence. Rather, it was that, looking familiarly asleep, he looked uniquely at peace.

We sat down next to his head and stroked and petted him and talked. I admired, once again, his well-shaped ears, his beautiful head and throatlatch, his open nostrils, his silky coat, his textbook front legs that raced fifty-two times, in addition to every other sort of equine athletic activity, and were as clean at twenty years old as the day he was born. I admired his big, round, hard feet.

But we didn't just talk to him and about him. We relaxed next to him, stroking and petting, and talking about other things, too. We felt the coolness of his flesh, and it was pleasant, not gruesome. We stayed with him long enough to recognize that he was not there, that this body was like a car he had driven and now had gotten out of. The mare watched us, but she, too, was calm.

Later, when I spoke to the manager of my other mares and foals, she told me that when a foal dies, you always leave it with the mare for a while—long enough for her to realize fully that it is not going to get up again, and to come to terms with that. I thought then that this is true of people, too. We have to experience the absence of life in order to accept it.

My friends know that I adored Mr. T. to a boring and sometimes embarrassing degree. I would *kvell* at the drop of a riding helmet about his every quirk and personal quality. He was a good, sturdy, handsome horse, and a stakes winner, but not a horse of unusual accomplishment or exceptional beauty. He was never unkind and never unwilling—those were his special qualities. Nevertheless, I watched him and doted over

him and appreciated him day after day for almost six years.

The result is a surprising one. I miss him less, rather than more. Having loved him in detail (for example, the feel of his right hind leg stepping under me, then his left hind, then his right hind again… for example, the sight of his ears pricking as he caught sight of me over his stall door… for example, the sight of him strolling across his paddock… for example, the feel in my hands of him taking hold and coming under as we approached a fence… for example, the sound of his nicker), I have thousands of clear images of him right with me. I think I miss him less than I thought I would because I don't feel him to be absent.

There is no way to tell non-horsey people that the companionship of a horse is not like that of a dog, or a cat, or a person. Perhaps the closest two consciousnesses can ever come is the wordless simultaneity of horse and rider focusing together on a jump or a finish line or a canter pirouette, and then executing what they have intended together. What two bodies are in such continuous, prolonged closeness as those of a horse and rider completing a hundred-mile endurance ride or a three-day event? I have a friend who characterizes riding as "one nervous system taking over another." I often wonder—which is doing the taking over, and which is being taken over?

I never expected to be writing this article. Rather, I intended, in twenty years, to write, "Oldest Known Equine Is Seventeen-Hand Ex-Racehorse." But I see it is time to take my own advice, the advice I gave my daughter when she got her first real boyfriend. I told her that no matter what happened with this boyfriend, once she had experienced the joys of a happy and close relationship, she would always know how to have that again, and would always have that again. And the truth is, that works for horses, too.

◆ ◆ ◆

WHY IS IT THAT GIRLS LOVE HORSES?

MAXINE KUMIN

◆ ◆ ◆

For the last 21 days—ever since the mare's milk bag filled and gradually grew brick-hard—I have slept with the intercom open, relaying every snort, yawn, cough, and chew into my waiting ear from 10 P.M. until dawn. Nightly I have laid out my clothes on the floor next to the bed, like a fireperson. I have leaped up nine times in three weeks, yanked on jeans, socks, boots, and hurled my half-conscious body downhill, across the road, over the snowbanks, into the barn. False alarms, all of them. Just yesterday nature out-witted me. The foal slipped silently into the world in his own time.

The annual foals are the best present of my middle age.

The best present of my childhood, a British storybook called *Silver Snaffles*, by Primrose Cumming, arrived on my tenth birthday. In this fantasy tale, a little girl walks through the dark corner of a draft-pony's stall into a sunlit world where articulate ponies with good English country-squire manners and highly individual personalities give lessons to eager youngsters. The story culminates in a joyous hunt staged by the foxes themselves, who are also great conversationalists. Jenny, launched as a rider, learns that she is to be given a pony of her own. Now she must relinquish her right to the magic password and to the dark corner of Tattle's stall, through which she has melted every evening

into a better world. I thought it the saddest ending in the history of literature.

By this age I had already begun to ride—an hour a week, one dollar an hour—on one of those patient livery horses who for most of their lives carry on their backs the timid and inept, the brash and graceless. Bob Ross of Ross-Del Riding Academy in Philadelphia, taught me how to post by riding so closely alongside old Charlie that he could keep one hand under my elbow and guide my risings and fallings in the saddle. Through Carpenter's Woods into Fairmont Park along Wissahickon Creek we rode decorously side by side. It was a safe excursion.

A year or two later, when I could wield a manure fork and manage a full-size wheelbarrow, I traded extra hours in the saddle for muckings-out, groomings, and the cleaning of worn school tack. It didn't especially matter to me whether I rode or not; I was happy just to be in the presence of horses. I wanted to inhale them, and I wanted them to take me in. Even though I had graduated to more challenging horses, I was happy just to perch on the top bar of Charlie's stall and admire him. I liked to watch the wrinkles on his muzzle crease as he chewed. Days that I wasn't allowed to walk two miles to the rental stable, I skulked abovestairs and reread *Silver Snaffles*.

Eventually, I wore this book out with ritual rereadings; somehow it disappeared from my life. When, 40-odd years later, I assumed my duties at the Library of Congress, it occurred to me that *Silver Snaffles* was undoubtedly housed in that enormous repository of knowledge. The day I found it in dusty stacks, I sat down on the marble floor and turned the familiar pages in disbelief. The book was real, after all! Then I carried it up to the Poetry Room that overlooks the Capitol and the Mall and read the story all over again, savoring the parts I had remembered verbatim, and wept.

I think I was crying for my lost childhood, but I'm still not sure. The cathartic effect of the book was not assuaged for me by Jenny's acquiring a pony of her own. Nothing would compensate for that loss of innocence, of the ability to speak the password and walk into a kingdom of virtue and honor. The deprivation that I felt when the female hero was denied continued access to Paradise was the loss of an intensity, a closeness for which I have no adequate words. This bonding, I believe, lies at the heart of horse fever.

For example, when my second daughter and her best friend were nine and 10 years old, they acted out elaborate scenarios involving plastic horses that were stabled in shoe boxes on bedding made of shredded newsprint. The horses had names, genders, and disparate personalities. "It had to do with thinking and feeling like a horse," she now says. "We could twitch our skin to shake off flies; we sucked water when we drank; and of course we pranced around a lot. It was better than ballet class."

This daughter is here for a visit during the last few weeks of her maternity leave. After the baby is fed and asleep in his carriage, she comes down to the barn while I muck stalls. She hauls the water buckets, rakes up loose hay, grooms the riding mares. Yes, she is still connected.

Such bonding is profoundly physical. We

learn our horses' body language and they learn to respond to a body language we use—body pressures and positions called aids—to ask for changes in gait and direction. I still remember how astonished I was to discover, riding bareback under instruction, that my horse would move continually at a trot in a small circle without any recourse on my part to reins so long as I kept my body pivoted in that direction and asked him to do so with the pressure of my calf on that same side. There are a variety of body signals the rider gives the horse that ask it to come forward onto the bit, to use its hind legs, to halt squarely, back up, move off at a trot or canter, and so on. None of these responses is achieved by magic; all require patient repetition and forbearance. One day there is a little breakthrough. Then, another and another.

At the risk of sounding sexist—some wonderful trainers and handlers are male—I believe that women work best with horses in certain situations. I have seen a pigtailed 10-year-old girl quiet a raving, 17-hand thoroughbred who had glimpsed out of the corner of his eye the vet's approach and was plunging around his stall in a full-scale tantrum. The youngster simply walked in, caught a piece of her friend's mane as he whirled past her, took a firm pinch hold on his neck skin, and slipped a halter over his nose before three male stable attendants with whips and twitches could agree on who was to undo the door latch.

Women's empathy, subtlety, ability to read the nuance of difference that leads to change; our gift of timing; our socializing as nurturers—all contribute to our considerable successes, for example, in the large thoroughbred and standard-bred breeding farm operations; in the show ring; as exercise riders, grooms, and jockeys in the racing world; and as instructors at levels ranging from the local day-camp riding program to professional training establishments.

Granted, other elements enter into the young woman's passion for horses, and developing a sexuality may be one of these. But the stereotyped concept that girl children long to sit astride the muscular power and rhythmic motion of a horse out of deep sexual urges, and that, in time, they redirect this prepubescent desire toward its natural object of fulfillment, the adolescent boy, has always seemed to me too facile to be trusted. In the American West, where the cow pony represents not only the freedom to explore a space, but also the means to develop such working skills as cutting and roping and such recreational skills as rodeo riding or barrel-racing, males are still in the majority. Eastern pony clubs and 4-H horse groups have been for the most part the purview of mothers, perhaps as an alternate to such opportunities as Little League, which has belonged for the most part to competitive fathers.

I further mistrust the Freudian concept because it does not adequately explain the substantial number of adult females who, despite their comfortable adaptation to sex roles involving marriage and child-rearing, continue to lease, own, care for, ride, and raise horses.

I do not blink at the fact that a horse often comes into a young girl's life at a time when she feels a need to take control in some measure of what is essentially an uncontrollable environment. The key factor is that an animal's responses can be counted on. When all else shifts, changes, and disappoints, the horse can remain her one constant. Her best friend may turn against her; fickle boys forget their admiration; siblings bicker with her; parents exact a too ardent fealty. Her favorite teacher may suddenly grow aloof. The violence of the real world, the threat of nuclear war, the poverty and deprivation she is at least peripherally and probably acutely aware of, all intensity her sense of adequacy to deal with these inequities. By comparison, the horse is predictable, manageable, kindly.

I asked Julia, my favorite 12-year-old working visitor, why she loves riding horseback. "It gives you a sense of freedom," she said. "You're sort of out of touch because you're higher up than everybody else." And then she added: "Taking care of horses makes you feel good because you're making somebody else feel

good. It's sort of a comforting feeling when you get done with the evening barn chores because you've put the horses away and you know you've made them feel cozy and secure."

The bond with horses, no matter its origin, is enjoyed ultimately for its own worth. I like to think that my own obsession serves a greater good. Living with horses reminds me daily of my place in nature. Tending them, training, riding or driving them links me with my tribal past. My mother, who was born before the automobile and electric lights and lived to her eighty-fourth year in a nuclear age, remembered with piercing clarity the names and dispositions of all the horses of her childhood in rural Virginia—the driving team, the plow horse, the hackney pony, the delivery wagon mules. In a way, then, I am keeping the faith, taking my rightful place in the continuum.

"The horse," Gervase Markham wrote in 1614, "will take such delight in his keeper's company, that he shall never approach him but the horse will with a kind of cheerful or inward neighing show the joy he takes to behold him, and where this mutual love is knit and combined, there the beast must needs prosper and the rider reap reputation and profit."

Cheerful or inward neighing is what I would cross-stitch on a sampler, if I were assigned to work one, as my mother was. Hers read, in the astonishing even stitches of a 12-year-old: *He maketh me to lie down in green pastures.* An appropriate piety, under the circumstances.

❖ ❖ ❖

FIRST RIDE

INGRID SOREN

◆ ◆ ◆

Henry Miller once said that a hero is a man who has conquered his fears. So watch me, wherever you are now. Perhaps I began to be a heroine when I sat on the back of a horse for the first time in my adult life. She as aptly named Dulcie, having the sweetest of temperaments and reputedly never a bad mood in her 19 years on the planet. Built like a table and standing 14.2 hands high, this sturdy Welsh cob tolerated my uneasy presence with the nobility of a gentle giant. Fearfully, I took in her wide chest, powerful shoulders, and the huge muscles of her chocolate-brown rump. Sitting astride her, I hung on with tense legs and tight hips, my shoulders and hands rigid, jaw locked, and embarked on my first hack ever across the English countryside.

We set off in the sleepy stillness of early afternoon in late August, under a windy sky. My sister rode alongside me on her pony, Tandy, a dainty creature of iron will and uncertain temper who eyed me with disdain as she picked her way along the tracks, conscious of her elegance but also of her strength. Of the two horses, she was the boss ever though she was sylphlike in comparison to the bulk of Dulcie. My sister was evidently concerned about the responsibility of taking a novice out into the lanes and tracks, but gave soothing replies to my anxious questions. She showed me how to hold the reins through my fourth and fifth fingers and instructed me to push my heels down and toes up. She had removed my sunglasses gently before we set out.

"But I always wear sunglasses," I protested.

"Not a very good idea," she suggested. She didn't say why, and only later did I realize that she didn't want to mention the subject of accidents. I acquiesced. She was the expert. I was in her hands, on her horse, and she had ridden for most of her life. It's funny: We are twins, but our interests and personalities had diverged at an early age.

We turned off the quiet lane from the paddock where she kept her horses into a tunnel of green that led through to the harvest fields. As Dulcie ambled along, I touched her strong neck with a sense of wonder and privilege that this massive animal would carry me on her back, bearing my weight with no protest. Her thick mane swung loosely to the rhythmic nod of her head as she walked, a fountain of coarse brown hair with auburn and straw-colored lights in it. I inhaled her horse scent, that delicious sweetness that I would come to love. She dropped her head to stretch her neck, and switched her ears sideways. I felt myself relax a little.

A pair of swallows swooped over the field as we emerged from the green lane. I remember a splash of scarlet pimpernel in the verge. As we walked alongside a hedge up a slope, the golden stubble exhaled the smell of harvest. A distant tractor rumbled around collecting bales of straw. The strong afternoon sun bleached the reaped fields, throwing shadows of hedgerow trees over the cut wheat.

At the top of the hill, we stopped to look back. Judith asked me how I was doing. I said I thought I'd gone to heaven: Never having seen the countryside from the back of a horse before, and being an avid walker and botanist, I was in my element. All around us lay expanses of ripened crops and stubble, punctuated only by viridian trees and lines of hedges. Swaths of corn alternated with darkly plowed earth in a far field, in brushstrokes that converged at the crest of the hill. Orange-tip butterflies flickered among rust-colored spikes of dock as Dulcie feigned starvation and made for some juicy leaves hidden in the grasses.

We rode for 2 hours that day (it seemed a much shorter time), walking mostly but with a couple of trots for which Judith prepared me in advance, offering rudimentary advice about

how to rise. "You're a natural," she said, at the end of the second one. Kind of her, I thought. Personally, I felt I had been bumping around in the saddle like a sack of potatoes with no control at all. Still, I appreciated her saying it.

My memories of that ride are paradoxically vague yet intense. What I do remember clearly, though, is that the next day, I thought I would never walk again. I was stiff; I was sore; I felt crippled. My sitz bones seemed to have pierced my bottom so painfully that I could only sit with care—and on something soft. I had thought I was a fit woman—an energetic walker, a yoga teacher even. I should be supple if anyone was, but riding had gotten to parts that even the most advanced asanas apparently had not. I felt as though someone had taken my legs, pulled them wide, and tried to split me up the middle.

But even this degree of discomfort did not put me off. That day in August proved to be the beginning of something that I could never have imagined for myself, because from childhood I had had a deep-seated fear of horses. Something woke up in me after that first ride, a dawning realization that the world is only a mirror of ourselves, and like Alice, I decided to walk through the looking glass.

◆ ◆ ◆

Begin Again

Melissa Holbrook Pierson

◆ ◆ ◆

My first riding lesson in more than twenty-five years was prefaced by an inadvertent scenic excursion lasting an hour and a half. The roads in this part of the country lack signs, for the most part, which would explain some of it; the rest was some garden-variety idiocy on the part of the driver. When at last I managed to find a telephone, which are in as short supply as road signs, I was crying in frustration. A thematic prelude to the act of taking up horseback riding again as an adult.

The advertisement that had led me down these circuitous roads read simply, "Learn to ride in harmony with the horse." Any more specificity would have been lost on me, who had last been instructed in "English"—meaning whatever saddle was around, on whatever horse was available. The only picture I possess of myself on a horse, from hundreds of hours spent thereon, shows me about to canter out of the frame, wearing bell-bottom jeans, hair flying, horse strung out and lacking any contact with the reins, and a smile of joy on my face; I was sitting on a saddle-seat saddle. I had also received jumping instruction at various points, sometimes with a forward-seat saddle and sometimes not. Needless to say, I do not know how to jump.

Luck and happenstance were about to deliver me to the place where I should have begun long ago, except that the world of riding has changed so much in the past quarter-century that the

option barely existed for children then: dressage, a systematic method of learning to ride on flat ground that consists of getting one's body in enough control that one is able to get the horse's body in control. This is not the official definition, assuredly, which is closer to teaching the animal to do under saddle and weight what it does without teaching in nature.

The brand-new red barn and indoor arena has an interior that owes something to a Gothic cathedral, with sprung wooden arches soaring to the roof. This is appropriate given the reverence with which the training of horse and rider is pursued within its precincts. I am met by Dominique, a woman my own age, with bobbed black hair and a subtly chipped front tooth; he body is slender but looks like it contains tensile springs just under the skin. When she starts talking, she doesn't stop. She explains here methodology, and why what she teaches is about working *with* the horse and his biomechanical capabilities. When she next moves on to the subject of intelligence, how it is something that will expand if you expect it to, I feel a sudden jolt: Yes! This is something I had come to understand, quite by accident, in the process of training my Border collie, whose intelligence seemed to grow the more she learned and discovered she was capable of it. It had struck me, beautifully, magisterially almost, as a model of *all* animal intelligence, including human. I wanted to say, "Yes, yes, it's true—you know, I believe . . ." but there was no place for me to say anything. No doubt as it should be.

As I mounted Dandy, a thirteen-year-old Quarter Horse whom I later came to call Saint Dandy for his dignity and intellect and forbearance of riders far stupider than he, a familiar but long-absent feeling washed over me: the desire to please the teacher. The almost crippling desire to please the teacher. It had been lying in wait, where it wanted to reconnect me instantaneously to a childhood memory that I would have preferred to remain forgotten. Suddenly it was present, not as a thought or a recollection but as an inhabitant of my being, reshaping me from the interior

like a Marvel comic-book character before I could even realize I should attempt to make it stop. It was the constancy of my semiconscious desire to hear the instructor say: "Wow, you have a *natural* talent for communicating with a horse." I had built entire castles in the sky on the foundation of this embarrassing wish as a child.

But the lesson of the lesson was to be the necessity of learning that there are no shortcuts, not with this horse business at any rate. It is plain hard work. I started to sweat under my borrowed hunt cap. I had walked in thinking I knew at least a little about riding; my knowledge lasted approximately six minutes. I was now down to zero. In subsequent lessons I would start mining a deficit. One solid bit of information that would stick conveyed the necessity at this age, for wearing a sports bra to sit the trot.

Near the end of the lesson, Dominique called out to me, "Now, I want you to think about stopping." I had already figured out that my former wisdom concerning stopping, usually

presented by my teachers as "Pull back on the reins," wasn't going to wash in this particular arena, not since notions of sense and weight and flow and breath and relaxation and lack of resistance had already been delivered as cornerstones of Dominique's methodology. So I did what she said. A voice inside my head whispered, "Stop," and that is all. Dandy took not one step more.

It was a miracle, and I reacted appropriately, sputtering and then sinking into bemusement. Dominique just smiled and nodded; the secret of this magic was old news to her. She went on to inform me that before the next lesson I would be well served by buying gloves, which would provide a more subtle feel of the reins, and proper breeches, which would help my seat. It knew it needed all the help it could get.

On the way home I kept replaying that moment when Dandy seemed to read my mind. If that was all it took to make a request, what, then, of all the horses whose mouths I had hauled on in the past? I had been taught to use a mace when a feather was the appropriate tool. And I had taught those horses—creatures that can feel you breathe, that can isolate the inch of skin on which a fly lands—that this is what life was like. The only protection they were to have was the power of the mind to dissociate from the body, and this they used until even a crop would draw forth only the detached look of someone who simple can't be bothered. Those were ghosts of horses. By now their bodies had been long dispatched to join their minds, wherever it is that worthy beasts go to find a freedom that lasts.

◆ ◆ ◆

ENGLISH RIDING, WESTERN STYLE

VICKI HEARNE

◆ ◆ ◆

In my dream life in those days I was in Vienna, Virginia, or England, about to introduce elegantly groomed and bred horses and their equally elegantly groomed and bred riders to the high arts of dressage and stadium jumping. But my eyes, once open, found it impossible to evade the hard, hot, high desert light and what it revealed—forty mongrel versions of dusty western tack on forty different versions of horse and puzzled western rider. While I was desperately trying to close the vast imaginative gap between the scenery of Twenty-nine Palms, presided over by Sand Mountain, and the white-fenced and well-ordered Arcadia of my dreams, a large red-shirted man ambled over to me.

"Reason I came here," he was saying, as if to himself, "we got this mare won't do nothing but jump out of her corral. But my little girl, that's Mary Pat, says she can ride Peggy, that's short for Pegasus because she won't stay in her corral—anyway, we heard maybe you could do something with her."

Escaping from her corral was Peggy's only distinction. Her mother was a hundred-dollar Indian pony from the Morongo Reservation, and her father was uncertain. But I agreed to look at her, and Mary Pat's father, Dave Nelson, signaled toward the group of horses, from which emerged an undersized mare with a more or less black, mottled coat. She was almost entirely hidden under sixty-plus pounds of roping saddle. On her back was Mary Pat, thirteen, anxiously clutching the reins and the saddle horn. There was nothing for it but to try the mare out, but my ignorant heart sank as I went to get my jumping saddle from the trunk of my car. I thought wistfully of the horses I could have in training if only I had a bit more money. If only I lived in Virginia. Or in England, or Europe, or in a different century and in another language and so on.

I headed Peggy toward an improvised jump made of stacks of old tires. She had never been asked to jump. Indeed, she didn't know the basic gaits—walk, trot, and canter—and she weaved and "squirreled," as horsemen say, seeking any avenue of escape, until she found that I was firm and that there was no escape.

So she jumped the tires. Simply folded up her knees like she was praying and jumped, demonstrating textbook form.

There I was, with a more I knew I could do anything with—but the owners! Mary Pat had never even seen a jumping saddle. Her father had no conception of what goes into the making of a show jumper. But there is a lot of heart in that family, apparently a hereditary condition, for Mary Pat started surprising me. She was the first student I ever had who actually *did what I told her to do.* Older trainers had warned me that there would be such students, but I hadn't believed them until now. Watching Mary Pat and Peggy alone in the California desert, I thought of the diary of one nineteenth-century traveler who had said of southern California, "The mountains cut the land off from sympathy

with the East." I sometimes felt that God was whispering things into the landscape, in the breathing of that child and that horse.

Then there was the day, very early in Peggy's career, when a Santa Ana was blowing. While she and Mary Pat were on a course of jumps, the wind had blown the second fence of one combination just far enough so that there was no room between them for a horse to manage a proper landing and takeoff. Any rider would have been forgiven for pulling up, but Mary Pat just got this *look* on her face and headed her little mare into that fence. Peggy took them both at once, as one fence.

After that, when we went to horse shows, instead of hearing snotty remarks about Peggy such as "I think a hunter should look like a hunter, don't you?" we heard a new sort of remark. Things like, "Watch out for that little girl in the blue coat on the Appy. She can jump that horse out of a box!"

One day, at the L.A. County Fairgrounds, Mary Pat and Pegasus came in first in a huge open jumper class against seasoned professionals. But Mary Pay was unhappy, depressed, frustrated, because even though they had won, her mare wasn't going right. I said reassuringly, "Cheer up. There are at least fifty pros here who would be delighted to be going home with the purse you won today!"

Mary Pat set her chin, glanced at me through angry tears, and said, "My *mare* isn't happy. You always told me that what mattered was the horse!" Pegasus seemed to agree. She nodded her head vigorously a few times and stuck her eye next to my eye, regarding me meaningfully.

I remembered Gervase Markham, a sixteenth-century thinker, who opens his treatise on riding by saying, "Of all creatures, the horse is the noblest."

♦ ♦ ♦

ALL THINGS BRIGHT AND BEAUTIFUL

JAMES HERRIOT

◆ ◆ ◆

Probably the most dramatic occurrence in the history of veterinary practice was the disappearance of the draught horse. It is an almost incredible fact that this glory and mainstay of the profession just melted quietly away within a few years. And I was one of those who were there to see it happen.

When I first came to Darrowby the tractor had already begun to take over, but tradition dies hard in the agricultural world and there were still a lot of horses around. Which was just as well because my veterinary education had been geared to things equine with everything else a poor second. It had been a good scientific education in many respects but at times I wondered if the people who designed it still had a mental picture of the horse doctor with his top hat and frock coat busying himself in a world of horse-drawn trams and brewers' drays.

We learned the anatomy of the horse in great detail, then that of the other animals much more superficially. It was the same with the other subjects; from animal husbandry with such insistence on a thorough knowledge of shoeing that we developed into amateur blacksmiths—right up to medicine and surgery where it was much more important to know about glanders and strangles than canine distemper. Even as we were learning, we youngsters knew it was ridiculous, with the draught horse already cast as a museum piece and the obvious potential of cattle and small animal work.

Still, as I say, after we had absorbed a vast store of equine lore it was a certain comfort that there were still a lot of patients on which we could try it out. I should think in my first two years I treated farm horses nearly every day and though I never was and never will be an equine expert there was a strange thrill in meeting with the age-old conditions whose names rang down almost from mediaeval times. Quittor, fistulous withers, poll evil, thrush, shoulder slip—vets had been wrestling with them for hundreds of years using very much the same drugs and procedures as myself. Armed with my firing iron and box of blister I plunged determinedly into what had always been the surging mainstream of veterinary life.

And now, in less than three years the stream had dwindled, not exactly to a trickle but certainly to the stage where the final dry-up was in sight. This meant, in a way, a lessening of the pressures on the veterinary surgeon because there is no doubt that horse work was the roughest and most arduous part of our life.

So that today, as I looked at the three year old gelding it occurred to me that this sort of thing wasn't happening as often as it did. He had a long tear in his flank where he had caught himself on barbed wire and it gaped open whenever he moved. There was no getting away from the fact that it had to be stitched.

The horse was tied by the head in his stall, his right side against the tall wooden partition. One of the farm men, a hefty six footer, took a tight hold of the head collar and leaned back against the manger as I puffed some iodoform into the wound. The horse didn't seem to mind, which was a comfort because he was a massive animal emanating an almost tangible vitality and power. I threaded my needle with a length of silk, lifted one of the lips of the wound and passed it through. This was going to be no trouble, I thought as I lifted the flap at the other side and pierced it, but as I was drawing the needle through, the gelding made a convulsive leap and I felt as though a great wind had whistled across the front of my body. Then, strangely, he was standing there against the wooden boards as if nothing had happened.

On the occasions when I have been kicked I have never seen it coming. It is surprising how

quickly those great muscular legs can whip out. But there was no doubt he had had a good go at me because my needle and silk were nowhere to be seen, the big man at the head was staring at me with wide eyes in a chalk white face and the front of my clothing was in an extraordinary state. I was wearing a 'gaberdine mac' and it looked as if somebody had taken a razor blade and painstakingly cut the material into narrow strips which hung down in ragged strips to ground level. The great iron-shod hoof had missed my legs by an inch or two but my mac was a write-off.

I was standing there looking around me in a kind of stupor when I heard a cheerful hail from the doorway.

'Now then, Mr. Herriot, what's he done at you?' Cliff Tyreman, the old horseman, looked me up and down with a mixture of amusement and asperity.

'He's nearly put me in hospital, Cliff,' I replied shakily. 'About the closest near miss I've ever had. I just felt the wind of it.'

'What were you tryin' to do?'

'Stitch that wound, but I'm not going to try any more. I'm off to the surgery to get a chloroform muzzle.'

The little man looked shocked. 'You don't need no chloroform. I'll haul him and you'll have no trouble.'

'I'm sorry, Cliff.' I began to put away my suture materials, scissors and powder. 'You're a good bloke, I know, but he's had one go at me and he's not getting another chance. I don't want to be lame for the rest of my life.'

The horseman's small, wiry frame seemed to bunch into a ball of aggression. He thrust forward his head in a characteristic posture and glared at me. 'I've never heard owt as daft in me life.' Then he swung round on the big man who was still hanging on to the horse's head, the ghastly pallor of his face now tinged with a delicate green. 'Come on out o' there, Bob! You're that bloody scared you're upsetting t'oss. Come on out of it and let me have 'im!'

Bob gratefully left the head and, grinning sheepishly moved with care along the side of the horse. He passed Cliff on the way and the little man's head didn't reach his shoulder.

Cliff seemed thoroughly insulted by the whole business. He took hold of the head collar and regarded the big animal with the disapproving stare of a schoolmaster at a naughty child. The horse, still in the mood for trouble, laid back his ears and began to plunge about the stall, his huge feet clattering ominously on the stone floor, but he came to rest quickly as the little man upper-cutted him furiously in the ribs.

'Get stood up straight there, ye big bugger. What's the matter with ye?' Cliff barked and again he planted his tiny fist against the swelling barrel of the chest, a puny blow which the animal could scarcely have felt but which reduced him to quivering submission. 'Try to kick, would you, eh? I'll bloody fettle you!' He shook the head collar and fixed the horse with a hypnotic stare as he spoke. Then he turned to me. 'You can come and do your job, Mr. Herriot, he won't hurt tha.'

I looked irresolutely at the huge, lethal animal. Stepping open-eyed into dangerous

situations is something vets are called upon regularly to do and I suppose we all react differently. I know there were times when an over-vivid imagination made me acutely aware of the dire possibilities and now my mind seemed to be dwelling voluptuously on the frightful power in those enormous shining quarters, on the unyielding flintiness of the spatulate feet with their rim of metal. Cliff's voice cut into my musings.

'Come on, Mr. Herriot, I tell ye he won't hurt tha.'

I reopened my box and tremblingly threaded another needle. I didn't seem to have much option; the little man wasn't asking me, he was telling me. I'd have to try again.

I couldn't have been a very impressive sight as I shuffled forwards, almost tripping over the tattered hula-hula skirt which dangled in front of me, my shaking hands reaching out once more for the wound, my heart thundering in my ears. But I needn't have worried. It was just as the little man had said; he didn't hurt me. In fact he never moved. He seemed to be listening attentively to the muttering which Cliff was directing into his face from a few inches' range. I powdered and stitched and clipped as though working on an anatomical specimen. Chloroform couldn't have done it any better.

As I retreated thankfully from the stall and began again to put away my instruments the monologue at the horse's head began to change its character. The menacing growl was replaced by a wheedling, teasing chuckle.

'Well, ye see, you're just a daft awd bugger, getting yourself all airigated over nowt. You're a good lad, really, aren't ye, a real good lad.' Cliff's hand ran caressingly over the neck and the towering animal began to nuzzle his cheek, as completely in his sway as any Labrador puppy.

When he had finished he came slowly from the stall, stroking the back, ribs, belly and quarters, even giving a playful tweak at the tail on parting while what had been a few minutes ago an explosive mountain of bone and muscle submitted happily.

I pulled a packet of Gold Flake from my pocket. 'Cliff, you're a marvel. Will you have a cigarette?'

'It 'ud be like givin' a pig a strawberry,' the little man replied, then he thrust forth his tongue on which reposed a half-chewed gobbet of tobacco. 'It's allus there. Ah push it in fust thing every mornin' soon as I get out of bed and there it stays. You'd never know, would you?'

I must have looked comically surprised because the dark eyes gleamed and the rugged little face split into a delighted grin. I looked at that grin—boyish, invincible—and reflected on the phenomenon that was Cliff Tyreman.

In a community in which toughness and durability was the norm he stood out as something exceptional. When I had first seen him nearly three years ago barging among cattle, grabbing their noses and hanging on effortlessly, I had put him down as an unusually fit middle-aged man; but he was in fact nearly seventy. There wasn't much of him but he was formidable; with his long arms swinging, his stumping, pigeon-toed gait and his lowered head he seemed always to be butting his way through life.

'I didn't expect to see you today,' I said. 'I heard you had pneumonia.'

He shrugged. 'Aye, summat of t'sort. First time I've ever been off work since I was a lad.'

'And you should be in your bed now, I should say.' I looked at the heaving chest and partly open mouth. 'I could hear you wheezing away when you were at the horse's head.'

'Nay, I can't stick that nohow. I'll be right in a day or two.' He seized a shovel and began busily clearing away the heap of manure behind the horse, his breathing loud and sterterous in the silence.

Harland Grange was a large, mainly arable farm in the low country at the foot of the Dale, and there had been a time when this stable had had a horse standing in every one of the long row of stalls. There had been over twenty with at least twelve regularly at work, but now there were only two, the young horse I had been treating and an ancient grey called Badger.

Cliff had been head horseman and when

the revolution came he turned to tractoring and other jobs around the farm with no fuss at all. This was typical of the reaction of thousands of other farm workers throughout the country; they didn't set up a howl at having to abandon the skills of a lifetime and start anew—they just got on with it. In fact, the younger men seized avidly upon the new machines and proved themselves natural mechanics.

But to the old experts like Cliff, something had gone. He would say: 'It's a bloody sight easier sitting on a tractor—it used to play 'ell with me feet walking up and down them fields all day.' But he couldn't lose his love of horses; the fellow feeling between working man and working beast which had grown in him since childhood and was in his blood forever.

My next visit to the farm was to see a fat bullock with a piece of turnip stuck in his throat but while I was there, the farmer, Mr. Gilling, asked me to have a look at old Badger.

'He's had a bit of a cough lately. Maybe it's just his age, but see what you think.'

The old horse was the sole occupant of the stable now. 'I've sold the three year old,' Mr. Gilling said. 'But I'll still keep the old 'un—he'll be useful for a bit of light carting.'

I glanced sideways at the farmer's granite features. He looked the least sentimental of men but I knew why he was keeping the old horse. It was for Cliff.

'Cliff will be pleased, anyway,' I said.

Mr. Gilling nodded. 'Aye, I never knew such a feller for 'osses. He was never happier than when he was with them.' He gave a short laugh. 'Do you know, I can remember years ago when he used to fall out with his missus he'd come down to this stable of a night and sit among his 'osses. Just sit here for hours on end looking at 'em and smoking. That was before he started chewing tobacco.'

'And did you have Badger in those days?'

'Aye, we bred him. Cliff helped at his foaling—I remember the little beggar came arse first and we had a bit of a job pullin' him out.' He smiled again. 'Maybe that's why he was always Cliff's favourite. He always worked Badger himself—year in year out—and he was that proud of 'im that if he had to take him into the town for any reason he'd plait ribbons into his mane and hang all his brasses on him first.' He shook his head reminiscently.

The old horse looked round with mild interest as I went up to him. He was in his late twenties and everything about him suggested serene old age; the gaunt projection of the pelvic bones, the whiteness of face and muzzle, the sunken eye with its benign expression. As I was about to take his temperature he gave a sharp, barking cough and it gave me the first clue to his ailment. I watched the rise and fall of his breathing for a minute or two and the second clue was there to be seen; further examination was unnecessary.

'He's broken winded, Mr. Gilling,' I said. 'Or he's got pulmonary emphysema to give it its proper name. Do you see that double lift of the abdomen as he breathes out? That's because his lungs have lost their elasticity and need an extra effort to force the air out.'

'What's caused it, then?'

'Well it's to do with his age, but he's got a bit of cold on him at the moment and that's brought it out.'

'Will he get rid of it in time?' the farmer asked.

'He'll be a bit better when he gets over his cold, but I'm afraid he'll never be quite right. I'll give you some medicine to put in his drinking water which will alleviate his symptoms.' I went out to the car for a bottle of the arsenical expectorant mixture which we used then.

It was about six weeks later that I heard from Mr. Gilling again. he rang me about seven o'clock one evening.

'I'd like you to come out and have a look at old Badger,' he said.

'What's wrong? Is it his broken wind again?'

'No, it's not that. He's still got the cough but it doesn't seem to bother him much. No, I think he's got a touch of colic. I've got to go out but Cliff will attend to you.'

The little man was waiting for me in the yard. He was carrying an oil lamp. As I came up to him I exclaimed in horror.

'Good God, Cliff, what have you been doing to yourself?' His face was a patchwork of cuts and scratches and his nose, almost without skin, jutted from between two black eyes.

He grinned through the wounds, his eyes dancing with merriment. 'Came off me bike t'other day. Hit a stone and went right over handlebars, arse over tip.' He burst out laughing at the very thought.

'But damn it, man, haven't you been a doctor? You're not fit to be out in that state.'

'Doctor? Nay, there's no need to bother them fellers. It's nowt much.' He fingered a gash on his jaw. 'Ah lapped me chin up for a day in a bit o' bandage, but it's right enough now.'

I shook my head as I followed him into the stable. He hung up the oil lamp then went over to the horse.

'Can't reckon t'awd feller up,' he said. 'You'd think there wasn't much ailing him but there's summat.'

There were no signs of violent pain but the animal kept transferring his weight from one hind foot to the other as if he did have a little abdominal discomfort. His temperature was normal and he didn't show symptoms of anything else.

I looked at him doubtfully. 'Maybe he has a bit of colic. There's nothing else to see, anyway. I'll give him an injection to settle him down.'

'Right you are, maister, that's good.' Cliff watched me get my syringe out then he looked around him into the shadows at the far end of the stable.

'Funny seeing only one 'oss standing here. I remember when there was a great long row of 'em and the barfins and bridles hangin' there on the stalls and the rest of the harness behind them all shinin' on t'wall.' He transferred his plug of tobacco to the other side of his mouth and smiled. 'By gaw, I were in here at six o'clock every morning feedin' them and gettin' them ready for work and ah'll tell you it was a sight to see us all goin' off ploughing at the start o' the day. Maybe six pairs of 'osses setting off with their harness jinglin' and the ploughmen sittin' sideways on their backs. Like a regular procession it was.'

I smiled. 'It was an early start, Cliff.'

'Aye, by Gaw, and a late finish. We'd bring the 'osses home at night and give 'em a light feed and take their harness off, then we'd go and have our own teas and we'd be back 'ere again afterwards, curry-combing and dandy-brushin' all the sweat and dirt off 'em. Then we'd give them a right good stiff feed of chop and oats and hay to set 'em up for the next day.'

'There wouldn't be much left of the evening then, was there?'

'Nay, there wasn't. It was about like work and bed, I reckon, but it never bothered us.'

I stepped forward to give Badger the injection, then paused. The old horse had undergone a slight spasm, a barely perceptible stiffening of the muscles, and as I looked at him he cocked his tail for a second then lowered it.

'There's something else here,' I said. 'Will you bring him out of his stall, Cliff, and let me see him walk across the yard.'

And watching him clop over the cobbles I saw it again; the stiffness, the raising of the tail. Something clicked in my mind. I walked over and rapped him under the chin and as the membrana nictitans flicked across his eye then slid slowly back I knew.

I paused for a moment. My casual little visit had suddenly become charged with doom.

'Cliff,' I said. 'I'm afraid he's got tetanus.'

'Lockjaw, you mean?'

'That's right. I'm sorry, but there's no doubt about it. Has he had any wounds lately—especially in his feet?'

'Well he were dead lame about a fortnight ago and blacksmith let some matter out of his hoof. Made a right big 'ole.'

There it was. 'It's a pity he didn't get an anti-tetanus shot at the time,' I said. I put my hand into the animal's mouth and tried to prise it open but the jaws were clamped tightly together. 'I don't suppose he's been able to eat today.'

'He had a bit this morning but nowt tonight. What's the lookout for him, Mr. Herriot?'

What indeed? If Cliff had asked me the

same question today I would have been just as troubled to give him an answer. The facts are that seventy to eighty per cent of tetanus cases die and whatever you do to them in the way of treatment doesn't seem to make a whit of difference to those figures. But I didn't want to sound entirely defeatist.

'It's a very serious condition as you know, Cliff, but I'll do all I can. I've got some antitoxin in the car and I'll inject that into his vein and if the spasms get very bad I'll give him a sedative. As long as he can drink there's a chance for him because he'll have to live on fluids—gruel would be fine.'

For a few days Badger didn't get any worse and I began to hope. I've seen tetanus horses recover and it is a wonderful experience to come in one day and find that the jaws have relaxed and the hungry animal can once more draw food into its mouth.

But it didn't happen with Badger. They had got the old horse into a big loose box where he could move around in comfort and each day as I looked over the half door I felt myself willing him to show some little sign of improvement;

but instead, after that first few days he began to deteriorate. A sudden movement or the approach of any person would throw him into a violent spasm so that he would stagger stiff-legged round the box like a big wooden toy, his eyes terrified, saliva drooling from between his fiercely clenched teeth. One morning I was sure he would fall and I suggested putting him in slings. I had to go back to the surgery for the slings and it was just as I was entering Skeldale House that the phone rang.

It was Mr. Gilling. 'He's beat us to it, I'm afraid. He's flat out on the floor and I doubt it's a bad job, Mr. Herriot. We'll have to put him down, won't we?'

'I'm afraid so.'

'There's just one thing. Mallock will be taking him away but old Cliff says he doesn't want Mallock to shoot 'im. Wants you to do it. Will you come?'

I got out the humane killer and drove back to the farm, wondering at the fact that the old man should find the idea of my bullet less repugnant than the knacker man's. Mr. Gilling was waiting in the box and by his side Cliff, shoulders hunched, hands deep in his pockets. He turned to me with a strange smile.

'I was just saying to t'boss how grand t'awd lad used to look when I got 'im up for a show. By Gaw you should have seen him with 'is coat polished and the feathers on his legs scrubbed as white as snow and a big blue ribbon round his tail.'

'I can imagine it, Cliff,' I said. 'Nobody could have looked after him better.'

He took his hands from his pockets, crouched by the prostrate animal and for a few minutes stroked the white-flecked neck and pulled at the ears while the old sunken eye looked at him impassively.

He began to speak softly to the old horse but his voice was steady, almost conversational, as though he was chatting to a friend.

'Many's the thousand miles I've walked after you, awd lad, and many's the talk we've had together. But I didn't have to say much to tha, did I? I reckon you knew every move I made, everything I said. Just one little word and you always did what ah wanted you to do.'

He rose to his feet. 'I'll get on with me work now, boss,' he said firmly, and strode out of the box.

I waited awhile so that he would not hear the bang which signaled the end of Badger, the end of the horses of Harland Grange and the end of the sweet core of Cliff Tyreman's life.

As I was leaving I saw the little man again. He was mounting the iron seat of a roaring tractor and I shouted to him above the noise.

'The boss says he's going to get some sheep in and you'll be doing a bit of shepherding. I think you'll enjoy that.'

Cliff's undefeated grin flashed out as he called back to me.

'Aye, I don't mind learnin' summat new. I'm nobbut a lad yet.'

◆ ◆ ◆

FOR LOVE OF HORSES

MRS. GEOFFREY BROOKE

◆ ◆ ◆

In 1930, Mrs. Dorothy Brooke, the wife of a distinguished British Cavalry officer, relinquished a life of comparative ease and social pleasure to search for and rescue from undescribable conditions, what remained of the 1914-1918 Army horses and mules, which sixteen years previously had been sold into "bondage" in Egypt, where they were put to work in the streets of the cities, in remote market villages, and in the stone quarries. Always hungry and therefore weak, over-loaded to a degree, lame, crippled, harness-galled, ill-shod, frequently blind, suffering intensely from perpetual thirst in extreme summer heat, and tormented by flies, these horses, though incredibly old, were still struggling along the streets and in the markets, and straining under the whip to move the stone carts in the quarries, when Mrs. Brooke arrived in Egypt with her husband. The following excerpts are from the book, For Love of Horses: Diaries of Mrs. Geoffrey Brooke, *Edited by Glendar Spooner.*

Although sixteen years had passed between the sale of the Army war horses and her husband's appointment as Brigadier commanding the Cavalry Brigade in Egypt in 1930, the fate of these horses had always haunted Mrs. Brooke. She "hated to remember but could not forget" and one of the first things she realised upon hearing of her husband's appointment to Egypt was the dreadful certainty that she must use this opportunity to try and discover if any of these horses were still alive.

Once she arrived in Egypt, she established the Old War Horse Fund, which gathered donations to purchase old war horses from their Egyptian owners. Once purchased, the horses were either boarded at the S.P.C.A. hospital or put down and put out of their misery.

Thursdays became "buying days," and here she describes what it was like to bring the horses to the hospital: *Although in that climate and after enforced waiting the poor old darlings first attack on the water was anything but leisurely, once having quenched their initial thirst they loved to stand by the trough, dipping their old noses into the water and sipping comfortably. Feeding is less of a business. Here are large quantities of fresh berseem (lucerne) daily, stacks of bedding and bins of bran. Running round the lines with clover and bedding takes up a fraction of the time spent in leading all those old decrepit horses to the water troughs.*

The worst cases, those too bad to keep one single necessary minute are destroyed the day of purchase. All the others are taken into the yards and given every possible comfort.

No sooner do they feel the deep straw beneath their feet than with creaking stiff old joints and hocks, they lower themselves carefully but ecstatically on to the glorious comfort they had never thought to feel again. With outstretched necks and legs they lie there in a sort of weary torpor.

One wonders how often they have dreamt of such peace. Undoubtedly for years after their original heartless sale they looked for the straw bedding to which they were accustomed from birth, the regular feeds and water. Animals are clock-like in their habits and one wonders how long it took to break the habit of years so that they no longer looked in vain. Feed times are peak periods to any animal—they are their only sense of security. Ever since the Army sold them, these horses have, when they were not working, stood on bare stone floors or hard concrete or mud in draughty ill-ventilated ramshackle sheds (and the winter nights in Egypt are piercingly cold). They have had a minimum for food and seldom enough water, sometimes none. Horses are noted for their long memories but now so dimmed are these by ill-nourishment and hopelessness, they frequently smell cautiously at the straw we give them before gradually it dawns upon them that here at last is a bed again!

The morning after the buying day was her Black Friday. On that day she had to face selecting the horses that had to be put down. This she did alone. The number averaged twelve a day in oder to be sure that there would be room for the next batch on the following Thursday. She tried to pick the worst cases first, leaving those who were still able to appreciate food, comfort, and kindness for a few days longer. Week after week, month after month, she did this job.

In her diary she says: It is heartbreaking business and one which I dread beyond all words. To see one suffering or starving horse gives all horse lovers a pain in the heart. Imagine being faced, day after day, with rows of such animals, each one more pitiful than the last. And in so many cases one can sense the remnant of a gallant spirit and a nervous anxiety as to what fate may yet befall them. So accustomed are they by now to the endless demands of their owners, they nervously prick an ear or roll an anxious eye when I approach which adds immeasurably to my own misery when I simply have to order the syce [hospital worker] to lead this one or that one out to a distant shed to be put down. If only a green English field would miraculously appear outside that blistering dusty yard, a field with shady trees and brook running

through it, what heaven it would be! If only I could say to the syce who is my fellow executioner, lead them into that field, let them lie down and roll to their heart's content, let them crop the sweet grass and drink the cool running waters, if I could have said that and left them there for even a week, I would not have minded quite so much. But to have to give the order—one after the other after the other and after only a few hours precious rest in a shed and with the dread of tomorrow still in their eyes—caused me infinite pain.

Every Thursday for nine months of the year for four years Dodo Brooke [as she was known] sat in that slum street—which has since become known as "The Street of the English Lady"—with the other members of the Buying Committee, watching the sad procession of old crocks passing before them. One or two of the Committee begged not to be asked to come unless urgently needed—they could not stand it. But Dorothy Brooke did not miss a single Thursday. That day was indelibly written on her heart. To sustain herself she used occasionally to cross the road and enter the

stables where animals already ransomed were stretched out on the straw. The look on these horses' faces gave her the strength to return to the Committee table and to resume the work.

After one such afternoon, she wrote the following in her diary: *Often that afternoon I left the Committee table and wandered into the stables for the pure joy it gave me to watch the old horses' faces. Long years ago they had given up all hope of enough food or water, of a kind word, or any chance at all of evading the ceaseless round of everlasting work accompanied by the blows from their owners' sticks. They shambled behind the syces with drooping heads and sunken eyes...*

Now, however, their lagging steps were directed with unaccustomed gentleness across the road and over the pavement to the double doors of the stables, thrown open to receive them. Here many paused and cocked an ear. Obviously distrustful of all interiors—as well they might be, judging by the sort of places in which for years they had been housed—they hesitated. But Gibson [the supervisor of the stables] was there waiting. A pat on the neck and a little persuasion from him and the old horses walked in. As their ill-shod misshapen hooves felt the deep tibben bed beneath them, there would be another doubting

unbelieving halt. Then gradually they would lower their heads and sniff as though they could not believe their own eyes or noses. Memories, long forgotten, would then return when some stepped eagerly forward towards the mangers piled high with berseem, while others with creaking joints, lowered themselves slowly on to the bed and lay, necks and legs outstretched. There they remained, flat out, until hand fed by the syces. Once down they stayed there, not attempting to get up for many hours.

I shall never forget the thankfulness in my heart as I watched them. The worst of our difficulties was behind us. Here we were at long last, running our own show with every detail under our own control. Every horse was carefully and understandingly cared for while the comfort and efficiency of our Stable compared to the open shed in the S.P.C.A. Hospital Yards, was an inestimable blessing in itself.

Each animal was given his own feed tin and all available syces and any volunteers joined in filling them. A mixture of barley meal and bran damped with hot water may not appear all that wonderful to those accustomed to keeping horses under proper conditions. But to these three-parts starved dog-weary old horses it was bliss. They had not seen or smelt a mash since they

My success was almost entirely due to the fact that word had gone round that I was mad. The mad 'sitt'
(lady) was the name I was known by, not only to every decrepit horse owner in Cairo but over a large part
of Egypt itself. To the minds of these men, anyone who would go to the lengths I did to hunt and buy the old-
est, lamest and most useless horses in the country in order to provide them with better stabling than some of the
racing establishments, feed them on berseem and bran mashes, bed them deep in straw and employ a large army
of syces to attend to them only with the admitted object of having them killed in a few days time, proved beyond
all shadow of doubt that I was very mad indeed.

Mrs. Dorothy Brooke

left the Army fifteen or more years ago. But they had not forgotten!

The smell of the warm bran was enough. Immediately shrill excited whinnies echoed to the rafters. Ears were pricked and incredibly aged faces with nostrils quivering turned on scrawny necks over bony harness-galled shoulders in an attempt to see what was going on. As each tin was filled the nibble syces seized one on each hand and rushed them to the horses, which by now were so desperate that the whole stable was filled with the sound of stamping hooves, the blowing of nostrils, shrill urgent whinnies, and anxious nickerings. As each tin was tipped into the mangers an old nose ubried itself in the steaming mash, and the stamping and whinneying ceased. Then the building was filled with the most soothing of all sounds to a horse lover—the rhythmic, contented munching of good food.

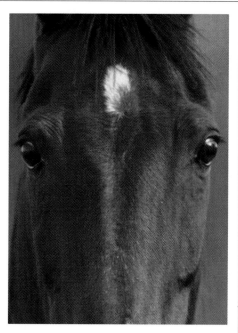

The blind horses—and there were many—received special attention, as did the old ladies and gentlemen who decided to go to bed as soon as they arrived—and to stay there. They were all fed mashes where they lay, their head supported by syces.

Those that were past enjoyment of any sort were put down at once. But at least they passed on to the sound of English voices, speaking kindly.

Gradually the surplus of old war horses which had accumulated while the work was held up, was absorbed; the numbers brought in for sale dwindled to an average of about forty to fifty every Thursday.

Looking back on all she had accomplished one can feel certain that she thought little of her own share and a great deal of other people's, for that was ever her way. She was indeed overwhelmed with gratitude to those who had

> *"So many people persist in giving me all the credit that I do want to make it abundantly clear that it would be absolutely impossible for me to achieve any fraction of success but for the unselfish, sustained and invaluable help rendered by a great number of other people, who never receive adequate recognition."*
>
> Mrs. Dorothy Brooke

made the rescue of the horses possible and it was no mean achievement. During the campaign from forty to seventy old war horses and mules were bought once a week during the nine months of the year for four years. For this purpose horse lovers in England and all over the world subscribed £40,000 in this time period alone, not counting what has been done since [in total, she rescued over 5,000 horses].

Imagine having to give instructions to put down twelve horses a day. Horses which all their lives had worked and which had had three or four blissful days only in which to realize that once again they had everything they could want to eat, good beds upon which to lay their weary bones, voices speaking kindly to them again—no heavy carts to drag after them day after day without even a Sunday's respite. Visualize having to make this decision, not once but for months and years, and in cold blood. The strain must have been very great, the heartache at times unbearable. It must have required a courage not often met with in men let alone in a woman. Especially a woman with a heart of gold.

◆ ◆ ◆

From the *Morning Post*, September 8, 1932:

OLD WAR HORSES

MRS. GEOFFREY BROOKE'S APPEAL

Mrs. Geoffrey Brooke, wife of Brig. Geoffrey Brooke, the authority on horse, is making a further appeal on behalf of the "Old War Horse Fund," of which she is hon. secretary. She writes:

"Not only Army horses, but those given up to their country by countless hundreds of patriotic people—favourite hunters, cherished friends of many families, born and bred in English fields—were at the close of the war sold to bondage in a foreign land. Fourteen long years of toil in the hands of strangers—in scorching sun, in sand, in a land where water is scarce, where flies are a torment, and where, owing to the poverty of their owners, the work has been far beyond their wasted strength! Many hundreds still survive, pleading for release—old, utterly weary, so deserving of a kindly redemption. 'Home' now can only be represented by a peaceful death, but what a release that is, what further suffering it saves!

"To save what remains of the thousands sold, the Old War Horse Fund has been organised, and a responsible committee formed in Cairo to purchase and humanely destroy these old war horses. The average price paid is about £7, for all these animals are bread-winners. Once bought, they are housed in the Fund's stables under English supervision. Their last hours are full of comfort and their end is painless.

"Will anyone who ever loved a horse and who can spare something, however small, help us to save them from their cruel servitude?"

An English branch of the fund has been opened at Lloyds Bank, Fleet, Hants, "Old War Horse Fund," at which contributions will be received. Correspondence concerning the work may be sent to the hon. secretary at this address.

A HISTORY OF HORSES
IN NORTH AMERICA

LISA DINES

❖ ❖ ❖

The horse as a species originated in North America, but prehistoric horses died out here thousands of years ago. No one is exactly certain why all the horses vanished from this continent. Other large land mammals, such as the saber-toothed tiger, mastodon, and woolly mammoth also became extinct at the same time.

After the horses vanished, huge herds of bison and antelope continued to flourish on the abundantly grassy plains where they had grazed beside the horses. Some say disease, others point to a change in climate from dust clouds after a meteor's impact, and still others say that being hunted to extinction by early man is the most probable cause of the horses complete disappearance from North America. Whatever the reason, no fossil remains of the horse have been found in North America dating past 7000 BC, and when the first European explorers came to the Americas in 1500 AD, the native people of that time had never seen horses.

Luckily, horses lived to reproduce in Europe and Asia after crossing the land bridge that existed between the two continents during prehistoric times. Three of the many (long-extinct) early horses were the Polish Forest horse, a massive, probably dapple-coated, draft-type horse with large hooves for walking over boggy ground; the Siberian Tundra horse, a small, thick-coated white pony; and the Oriental horse, small and graceful with possibly a dished face.

For many thousands of years, horses were eaten—not ridden. Cave paintings found in France from the Later Stone Age (about 40,000 to 8,000 BC) show horses (with short black legs, black tails, and upright black manes) pierced with arrows. During the New Stone Age (from about 6,000 to 3,500 BC) people began to grow crops such as wheat and barley instead of gathering wild plants, and raised animals such as pigs, sheep, and goats for food rather than following the wild heards from place to place. They constructed stone or mud-brick houses, but still considered the horse only a large game animal.

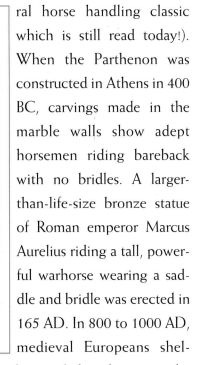

Finally, artwork shows horses pulling wheeled chariots containing soldiers or hunters in the Early Dynastic Period (around 2700 BC). From approximately 500 BC, Greek pottery depicts bareback riders with bridled steeds, and chariots pulled by horses participating in funeral processions, games, and races. In approximately 450 BC, the Athenian general and horseman, Xenophon, wrote *The Art of Horsemanship* (a natural horse handling classic which is still read today!). When the Parthenon was constructed in Athens in 400 BC, carvings made in the marble walls show adept horsemen riding bareback with no bridles. A larger-than-life-size bronze statue of Roman emperor Marcus Aurelius riding a tall, powerful warhorse wearing a saddle and bridle was erected in 165 AD. In 800 to 1000 AD, medieval Europeans sheltered both themselves and their horses in the same wooden barns.

The horse had at last become an important partner and friend to man, far too useful just to

eat. From then on, horses were selectively bred for qualities such as size, speed, and appearance. By the 1500s, horse breeds such as Arabs and Barbs were created in the Middle East and Africa, and the larger Andalusian warhorse was bred in Spain. From 1600 to 1800, a combination of these types, known simply as the "Spanish Horse" or the "jennet," was popular all across Europe.

Horses finally "returned" to the Americas when the Spanish explored and started to settle North America in the 1500s. They established breeding ranches in the Southwest territories from 1600 to 1700. The Spanish horses that escaped, were turned loose, or stolen established feral herds that became quite large in North America. A wild horse was called a "mesteno" or "mestango," which was Anglicized to "mustang."

Today, most American Mustangs are the result of breeding between the original, faster, leaner, "hotter" jennets, and larger, calmer, draft breeds such as the Percheron, Belgian, Clydesdale, or larger, more refined

Thoroughbred and carriage horses introduced over the years by ranchers, farmers, and the U.S. cavalry. Still existing today are just a few isolated "purer" herds which were not crossed with those of settlers or the cavalry. When genetically tested, they prove to have more "original Spanish" DNA and less resemblance to introduced breeds.

Due to the large expanse of grasslands, horses successfully fit back into the ecosystem in North America. Early American settlers deliberately added domestic stallions and mares to free-roaming herds to "improve" the size or quality (from which the settlers could capture new youngsters later), and settlers' domestic horses joined mustang herds after being freed by raids or destruction. For all of these reasons, by the 1860s, *two million mustangs* covered the plains of the United States. The largest wild-horse range of all was in Texas where grazing herds reportedly stretched for twenty miles at a time.

Despite this abundance, however, few people were interested in capturing and taming wild horses. They were considered difficult to catch and troublesome to train. Pure mustangs were thought by settlers and ranchers to be too small for plowing, cattle roping, or driving. The Native American tribes had already traded or stolen enough horses from the Spanish to be well-equipped by the end of the 1700s. For all of these reasons, huge herds of mustangs continued to graze unhindered in many western states. In the early 1900s, even more horses were added to the mustang herds when farmers and ranchers abandoned them during the Great Depression, and as the demand for horses was greatly reduced due to the invention of the automobile and tractor.

◆ ◆ ◆

Wild Horse Annie

♦ ♦ ♦

One day in 1950, Velma B. Johnson was driving in Nevada and noticed a truck in front of her with blood dripping from the back. She followed the truck and discovered that it was carrying horses to a slaughter house.

Johnson began to conduct her own research into how wild horses were rounded up by "mustangers"—ranchers and hunters that captured wild horses for slaughter. It was then she became aware of the extent of inhumane treatment of wild horses throughout the America west.

She wrote "Although I had heard that airplanes were being used to capture mustangs, like so many of us do when something doesn't touch our lives directly, I pretended it didn't concern me. But one morning in the year 1950, my own apathetic attitude was jarred into acute awareness. What had now touched my life was to reach into the lives of many others as time went on."

Determined to make a difference, Johnson began a grassroots campaign. The campaign first captured the attention of school children.

Children from all across America began sending letters to newspapers and legislators and attracted enormous attention that outraged the public and made then aware of the issue. And, as public attention grew, some of Johnson's critics began to call her wild Horse Annie, and the name stuck.

But no matter what her critics did, newspapers continued to publish articles about the

exploitation of wild horses and burros. By July 15th, 1959 the Associated Press wrote, "Seldom has an issue touched such a responsive chord."

In January 1959, Nevada Congressman Walter Baring introduced a bill prohibiting the use of motorized vehicles to hunt wild horses and burros on all public lands. The House of Representatives unanimously passed the bill which became known as the "Wild Horse Annie Act." The bill became Public Law 86-234 on Sept. 8, 1959.

However, this law did not include Annie's recommendation that Congress initiate a program to protect, manage and control wild horses and burros. Public interest and concern continued to increase, and with it came the realization that federal management, protection, and control of wild horses and burros was essential.

In response to the public outcry, members of both the Senate and the House introduced a bill in the 92nd Congress to provide for the necessary management, protection and control of the wild horses and burros. The Senate unanimously passed the bill on June 19th, 1971. After making some revisions and adding a few amendments, the House also passed the bill by a unanimous vote. It became known as the Wild Free-Roaming Horse and Burro Act of 1971.

◆ ◆ ◆

WHY DO PEOPLE LOVE HORSES?

LISA DINES

◆ ◆ ◆

There is a saying that goes: *The outside of a horse is good for the inside of a man.*

The sight of a horse peacefully grazing in a field can make many people think of kindness, softness, and safety—and for those of us who ride, we are immediately reminded of being powerfully transported far above the ground on a strong, gentle back. We are awed by the athletic power, beauty, and grace of horses, and entertained by their costumed riders. We are fascinated by stories of legendary equines who survived hardship or performed heroic feats, by those who touched their owners deeply or made them proud (and occasionally rich). Some of us are reminded of the "old days" before the combustion engine when horses were an indispensible part of our livelihoods and our lives.

Most of us have never encountered a "rogue" or vicious horse. The bucking broncos at the rodeo are for entertainment, far removed from lesson or camp horses we have loved and learned from, trail or dude ranch mounts we have rented and enjoyed on our vacations. We are continually amazed when meeting horses that despite their size and power, they are affectionate and sweet, and grateful for their feed and care.

There will always be a part of us that needs to be with other animals, and the horse is unequalled as a closely-knit partner capable of carrying us away for fun and adventure.

◆ ◆ ◆

Permissions Acknowledgments

Dickens, Monica. From *Talking of Horses*, by Monica Dickens. Copyright © 1973 by Monica Dickens (Text); Copyright © 1973 by William Heinemann Ltd. (Illustrations). By permission of Little, Brown and Company, Inc.

Dines, Lisa. "A History of Horses in North America" from *The American Mustang Guidebook* by Lisa Dines. Copyright © 2001 by Lisa Dines. Reprinted by permission of Willow Creek Press.

Dines, Lisa. "Why Do People Love Horses" from *Why Horses Do That* by Lisa Dines. Copyright © 2003 by Willow Creek Press. Reprinted by permission of the Publisher.

Haas, Jessie. "Ride Back With Me," from *Hoofprints: Horse Poems* by Jessie Haas. Copyright © 2005 by Jess Haas. Used by permission of HarperCollins Publishers Inc.

Hearne, Vicki. "English Riding Western Style," from *Animal Happiness* by Vicki Hearne. Copyright © 1994 by Vicki Hearne. Reprinted by permission of HarperCollins Publishers Inc.

Herriot, James. From *All Things Bright and Beautiful* by James Herriot. Copyright © 2004 by the author and reprinted by permission of St. Martin's Press, LLC.

Kumin, Maxine. "Why Is It That Girls Love Horses" from *Ms.* (April 1983). Copyright © 1983 by Maxine Kumin. Reprinted by permission of the author.

Markham, Beryl. "Was There a Horse with Wings" from *West With The Night* by Beryl Markham. Copyright © 1942, 1983 by Beryl Markham. Reprinted with permission of North Point Press, a division of Farrar, Straus and Giroux, LLC.

Page, Margot. "The Allure of Horses" from the Introduction of *Just Horses* by Margot Page. Copyright © 1998 by Margot Page. Reprinted by permission of Willow Creek Press.

Pierson, Melissa. "Begin Again," from *Dark Horses And Black Beauties* by Melissa Pierson. Copyright © 2000 by Melissa Holbrook Pierson. Used by permission of W.W. Norton & Company, Inc.

Smiley, Jane. "Mr. T's Heart," from *Practical Horseman* (October 1999). Copyright © 1999 by Jane Smiley/Horse Heaven. Reprinted by permission of the Aaron M. Priest Literary Agency, Inc.

Soren, Ingrid. "First Ride" from *Zen and Horses: Lessons From a Year of Riding*. Copyright © 2002 by Ingrid Soren. Reprinted by permission of Rodale, Inc.

Spooner, Glenda, Ed. *For Love Of Horses: Diaries of Mrs. Geoffrey Brooke*. Copyright © The Brooke Hospital for Animals, Cairo, British Columbia House. Reprinted with permission.